TAX TREES

SAVING THE

UNITED STATES

TAX TREES

SAVING THE

UNITED STATES

by

Robert Robinson

A Bible of Booklets

Vol. 1, Ed. 1

INTRODUCTION

<u>Saving the United States</u>

"The handbook that teaches Native Americans how to save the United States, take back their country and banish the non-native traitors forever!"

Dedication

My work is dedicated to the indigenous people of the English-speaking world yearning to break free from the idiotic foreign imperialists currently occupying their homeland. These Germanic civilizations are destroying our countries with runaway government spending and persecuting nationalistic patriotism.

To all the aboriginal tribes inhabiting the New World, South Africa, Oceania and Siberia: This book is for you! Don't let leftists dismantle your industries and take away your right to resist them. It's time to take the power back!

Foreword

As a Native American, I've known Robert since he was a young boy. I first met him while I was working at his late stepfather's tax business. From my own personal experience, this man truly is an honest, trustworthy, born-again, Sabbatarian Christian. What he lacks in formal education he more than makes up for in sheer firsthand experience, work ethic and authentic moral character.

This dilemma we're facing is a national security issue of the highest degree. You need to follow these handbooks' directions ASAP! If you don't, Western Civilization falls forever! TAX TREES is the only plan guaranteeing freedom.

-Nancy Davis

Preface

Saving the United States is the first volume of the TAX TREES trilogy. It teaches Native Americans how to fix their governments and deport the idiots bleeding the Free World dry. Bible of booklets is a homonym, or a play on words. It was inspired by the Holy Bible, itself a compilation of numerous books. What began as a forestry research project evolved into something far superior!

Several dissolved booklets were merged together to create this handbook. Defunct titles include Saving the Governments, How to Pay Off $18.5tril of National Debt in 24 hrs. and The Landscaper's Bible. I wanted to save my country, so I hope you'll enjoy over 10+ years of my hard-earned work!

Robert W. Robinson, Jr.

-Author, TAX TREES

TABLE OF CONTENTS

Synopsis
Mission Briefing

Manifesto

America is being destroyed by its national debt caused by runaway government spending. Currency devaluation, illegal immigration, outsourced manufacturing, price gouging and fire suppression within ecosystems also pose problems. The culprit: Imperialist squatters! You must act now before it's too late! We cannot defeat them through war; you've already tried that and lost. Starting another one brands us as traitors. Instead, we can outcompete them through commerce – financial warfare!

White Wolf

If we take away their money, you gain complete control over them. Then, we can lure them overseas by giving them jobs. Yet, it'll be easier said than done. You'll need to collaborate with other tribes in every English-speaking country. Additionally, my plan takes three generations to complete. Capitalize on the stupidity; they rarely read nonfiction and aren't smart enough to understand what TAX TREES really is about!

Preview

Chapters following Operation White Wolf have been grouped into four, unequally-sized quadrants. Each one is marked by a different picture visible on their chapters' title pages. The first covers executive cabinets with balanced budgets. Next, is an affordable military inventory. Quadrant III harbors global defense strategies. A final quarter tackles privatizing our park systems. All 15 contain overviews and reviews. Overviews are key to unlocking my intel. Without them, you wouldn't understand anything. Reviews show readers how to apply this knowledge to the real World.

CHAPTER ONE

Operation White Wolf

<u>Call to Arms</u>

Listed below is this chapter's section directory. Topics are grouped together in subsections labeled by underlined bullets. Any further subdivision of information is organized into verses marked by bolded bullets.

Overview

Revolution

Global Coalition:

Assemble a global coalition of natives from the United States, British Commonwealth, South Africa, Oceania, Caribbean, Siberia and Tibet! Siberians and Tibetans strike trade deals with governments to garner support for mutual benefit relationships. Inform British and Irish nationalists we're trying to deport their idiots, not overthrow their civilizations. Ask them to prevent these exiles' families from obtaining tourist rights. Never forget the remnants of each race inhabiting your land who support you!

Financial Warfare:

Establish family-owned and operated businesses. To avoid discrimination lawsuits from only hiring natives, companies form employee associations. The first generation begins their assault in rural outskirts. Your second creates a mirror-image economy to undercut pink-collar services in towns and city suburbs. A final wave infiltrates white-collar corporate HQs along skylines. All three acquire funds before breeding families with up to seven children to achieve a population not exceeding 120 million.

Remnant

Two Betrayals:

U.S. Democrats seek to eradicate personal freedom and Christian values. Republicans recklessly increase military spending and neglect the needy. Unfortunately, we must swing support across current party lines to restore political balance in the Free World. Doing so blocks future bills and forces these tyrants to enact our proposals instead. We need to begin paying down the national debt long before this plan is complete.

Throwing Copper:

Wait to pass legislation to revoke their citizenships, green cards, work VISAs and tourist rights on Thanksgiving. Send them adrift to forever inhabit an accursed bad land, like they did to your people. Never again shall they wield any power over us!

Political Science

Provocation

Historical Negation:

First Nations saved the lives of weary pilgrims ever since Roanoke by serving as our guides. They let us live freely amongst their own, yet we're taught we had to relocate them to make room. Coalitions of warriors and French privateers fought alongside our Continental forces. We wouldn't have won the war otherwise. Colonies drafted treaties asking peace, but they were concocted to deceive allied tribes into forfeiting land. Before they attacked us, we killed their women and children. Cities larger and more advanced than London used to exist, yet we always held an air of superiority.

Persecution

U.S. Democrat Party:

I'm a Southern man and lived most of my life in rural small towns throughout the early 2000s. I've worked for many racist, right-wing Dixiecrats ripping others off. While hanging out with friends in a rural low-income neighborhood, the KKK barged in. At the time, I was a mob boss tasked with arbitration between local gangs. My late stepfather didn't work for the Italians, but neither did the Mexican, Russian or Chinese Mafias. I was informed about their primary purpose: Keeping the Democrat Party strong! Any self-respecting minority should view voting for them as treason!

Southern Strategy:

KKK membership peaked at six million. This organization brainwashed white people into believing they were protecting them and black people were the enemy. Once their true colors as a terroristic hate group were exposed, Southern evangelical conservatives shifted support to MLK's Republican Party. Urban minorities were fooled into believing all rural conservatives are these racist bigots and persecuted them. Backstabbed Republicans grew prejudice towards them and stopped helping them. Doing so only fueled further ignorance between both demographic groups.

McCarthy Scare:

European Democrats parallel U.S. conservatives. Australian Liberal Party members are center-right nationalists. However, American liberals are tyrannical leftists. They don't represent what classical liberalism is in any form at all. Instead of accepting the majorities' will ever since 1958, which is the definition of what democracy is, they sought to replace us with another population to remain in control –high treason!

Sabotage

Cold War Socialism:

NAZI is the acronym National Socialist Workers' Party proving fascism is right-wing socialism. USSR stands for Union of Soviet Socialist Republics showing communism is left-wing socialism. Furthermore, most Nordic countries are just liberal democracies (classical liberalism, not leftism), not socialist nations. These dictatorships trick useful idiots to support them in hopes of easy gain only to install regimes for themselves. Stealing from the industrious leads everyone to poverty. It defeats the purpose of trying to work harder and become more educated. Don't try to deny their genocides!

Totalitarian Centralization:

Marxism rebranded itself Leninism, then Stalinism and finally, modern communism. Conservatives were forced to pit one regime against another throughout most of the 20th century. Latin America, Africa and Asia were dominated by dictatorships. Doing so garnered flak from Dems. American liberalism followed suit as progressivism, populism and globalism. Hollywood celebrities went from champagne socialists to limousine liberals. Those elitists sold their souls and seek to destroy Christian values.

Writing on the Wall:

President LBJ's welfare quote is, "I'll have those niggers voting Democrat for the next 200 years!" I knew a WWII veteran named Wayne Guthrie. He grew up on a farm along FM 1960 in Houston, TX. LBJ's men shot some of his family's cattle to control the meat market. Ever since the '70s, publicly-held companies and nonprofits were infiltrated by Dems poisoning them to achieve support from special interest groups.

Idiocracy

Political Correctness:

Feminism lost all credibility after its first two waves. Social justice warriors (SJWs) demonize others so they can be viewed as a hero to those they've deemed victims. Blindly-defending womankind is white knighting and any minority is virtue signaling.

Labor Parties:

Labor parties are left-wingers claiming to protect its working-class citizens. Reducing currency devaluation, not raising minimum wage, is the answer. Green parties are more liberal, but too incompetent to pose a threat. Don't support their nonsense!

U.S. Republican Party:

White supremacists retained fat retinues of Dixiecrats. However, remaining factions of fascists corrupted the GOP. Runaway defense spending and warmongering dating back to WWI created most of our national debt. WWII's bailout added tremendous debt and prevented us from learning how to live responsibly across two centuries.

Town & Country

Municipalities

Social Services Networks:

Cities provide services towns cannot due to their superior economic prowess. Many handicapped, retarded, senile and elderly depend on them to survive. Without a center-left lean, local governments would grow too minimalistic to offer the needy proper assistance. Conservative suburbanites shall swing polls to prevent states from becoming left-wing. Until the Constitution Party grows powerful enough to rival the Grand Old Party, always throw support to federal and state Republican candidates.

The Libertarian Party:

Libertarians failed to achieve mainstream status because they marketed themselves as another conservative party. Instead of dividing the current conservative voice, they should redirect their focus as an alternative to the U.S. Democrat Party. They combine fiscal conservatism and social liberalism, not left-wing American liberalism.

Suburban Swing:

Establish future strongholds by returning greener petrochemical and manufacturing jobs to inner cities. Offering employees non-voting preferred stock (corporate) and preferred interest units (partnerships) renders trade unions obsolete! Libertarians can win elections by earning conservative support in the suburbs. Constitutionalists swing votes from center-left independents dwelling in remote micropolitan regions.

Townships

Community Support:

Towns lack government assistance because they're less affluent, way too spread out across vast swaths of land to sustain public transits besides private sector bus routes and sparsely-populated. Most countryfolk developed strong, close-knit communities of neighborhoods and families to support one another. Locals are forced to conserve resources in the absence of pay increases. Thus, explaining their center-right leaning.

The Constitution Party:

Apply similar principles to swing votes. Throw support behind the GOP if their county populations are still straight-red. Otherwise, the Dems would win. Furthermore, town dominated by natives are free to elect any Taxpayer Party candidate! Suburban forces swing whenever it's necessary while our urban vanguard leans Libertarian.

Review

Resistance

Okhotskian Federation:

Encourage Russia to colonize Siberia by creating two neutral countries: Okhotskia and Tunguska! In exchange for their freedom, they give the Russians a cut of its natural resources. Grant Okhotskia the western banks of Yenisei River and Lake Baikal, an Arctic corridor linking all islands east of the Urals, its southern mountain ranges and anything eastward. Evenki forfeit minor land tracts, but no other tribe loses anything! Okhotsk City is the republic's capital. Russian military bases protect both countries.

Kingdom of Tunguska:

Tunguskans get the remaining portions of the Western Siberian Plain and Central Siberian Plateau. Remap Krasnoyarsk Krai and Irkutsk Oblast according to fall lines or watersheds. Krasnoyarsk City serves as its capital. Okhotskians control an aqueduct connected to Lake Baikal supplementing additional potable water sold as needed.

Renaissance

Federated Republics:

Yukon (Yukon Territory, Northwest Territories, BC, Alberta, Saskatchewan, Manitoba) declares independence. Alaska breaks off the U.S. while Puerto Rico becomes a state so we can maintain 50 stars in its flag. Greenland acquires Nunavut, but Iceland and Svalbard remain unaffected during this transition. Australia goes the route of South Africa by electing a president, yet both can remain part of the British Commonwealth.

Island Commonwealths:

New Zealand transforms into a kingdom and establishes a commonwealth amongst its Polynesian brethren. The Dominican Republic is where Taino people unite the Caribbean. The remaining two countries are federations: Papua New Guinea unifies Melanesia. The Federated States of Micronesia annexes Gaum as its subordinated state, declares Hagåtña its federal capital district and merges Micronesia together.

CHAPTER TWO

Limited Government

<u>Quadrant 1:1</u>

Listed below is this chapter's section directory. Topics are grouped together in subsections labeled by underlined bullets. Any further subdivision of information is organized into verses marked by bolded bullets.

Overview

Liberation

Draining the Swamp:

Imagine 484 representatives splitting into 22 standing committees, each with 22 members. Some countries have up to 30 per body! Dividing each into two select subcommittees gives you 11-man tables. Private sector organizations can send their chairmen (corporate) and managing partners (partnerships) to speak to them. Give corporations boards of nine and partnerships seven! Stock corporations' C-suites and nonprofits' E-suites elect seven chief officers. Division cabinets (V-level) house five members while district management teams (D-level) are comprised of threes. U.S. Congress would have far fewer joint committees, board members and bureaucracy!

Flattened Bureaucracy:

Historically, George Washington's cabinet only had four departments: State, Justice, Defense and Treasury. Their parliamentary monarchial equivalents are dubbed as ministries. Limit each 2-5 subsidiary organizations. Civilian contractors, freelancers and military auxiliaries shall fulfill any other role the forementioned can't complete on their own. Prisoners, unemployed and vagrants can lend a hand too. Privatizing unnecessary public groups prevents their employees from being laid off. From my personal experience, giving leaders more than 12 subordinates overwhelms them.

Emancipation

Tribal Sovereignty:

Indigenous tribes continue to exist as "de jure" governments until Operation White Wolf is completed. Afterwards, they'll reincorporate as our future political parties electing political candidates for government office! The federal language shall remain English and each party is allowed to fly their own flag and/or coat of arms. This allows Native Americans to rapidly coordinate leadership and communication between the 2,000 languages spoken between tribes. Previous generations lacked this capacity. Maybe, Manifest Destiny turned out to be the natives' ultimate weapon after all!

Balanced Budgets

Liquidation

National Revenue: $5.5 trillion

Federal, state and local governments receive $5.5t off taxation, treasuries and bonds. Current spending plans still garner annual deficits. Until we pay off the national debt, our combined governments can't enact a 10% flat tax and must live off savings bonds.

Libertarian Privatization: $3 trillion

Privatize Social Security, Medicare, Medicaid and USPS. Park co-os operated by businesses purchase 99% of government-owned land and are inspected by rangers. Doing shrinks public sector work forces down to 1.4mil federal, 2.6mil state and 5.2mil local employees. That's ½ the overhead! Doing so adds another $3t annually.

Civilian Conservation Corps: $892 billion

State unemployment programs require participants to remove litter, invasive species and execute seasonal burns along roadways. Vagrants labor underneath bridges and along channels to restore bottomland ecosystems according to my forestry models. Additionally, giving them loitering rights renders homeless shelters totally obsolete!

Allied Arms Deals: $1.5 trillion

As of 2024, each service branch has roughly $500bil in fixed assets. My military only requires $115bil! All they have to do is upgrade old designs using the companies I've listed in this book's chapters! Lend-lease programs amongst reputable allies and cannibalization of existing parts eliminates any future procurement costs or the need to allocate foreign aid to other countries. Enact an annual defense budget of $300bil.

Military Personnel: $584 billion

Maintaining 258k actives, 258k reserves and 16mil civilians in draft pools frees at least another $500bil each year. Civilian contractors form auxiliaries, something the USSR lacked in WWII. That's why the Red Army recruited up to 35 million personnel!

Realty Divestment: $582 billion

Auction off unnecessary offshore military bases back to their own populace. Privatize 99% of park lands to private park co-ops, themselves governed by deputy rangers. Private sector organizations sublease land out to industry and camp organizations.

Annual Revenue = $10 trillion

Executive Cabinet

Homeland Security (540,000 members)

State Embassy Administration: (140,000 members)

This shall be the new Department of State! The secretary of state is head over the Dept. of Homeland Security. Their ambassador-at-large manages this administration.

Parks & Wildlife Administration: (40,000 members)

Department of Interior folds into my DPW. Federal parks become state run. Minerals Division handles mining concerns, Land Mgt. permits and Water Mgt. wetland issues. Tolled park routes are separate navigational systems from the TSA's FHWA roadways.

Transportation Security Administration: (80,000 members)

TSI conducts airport security screening, air marshals ride planes undercover and sea marshals ride cruise ships. ATF issues permits and FHWA repairs current roadways.

National Intelligence Administration: (260,000 members)

Represented by an ODNI emblem. Secret Service guards presidents, NSA monitors communications and Cyber Security blocks hackers (NGA emblem). NASA charges civilian companies to cover the expenses of maintaining their GPS satellites for them!

National Energy Administration: (20,000 members)

EPA controls pollution, Strategic Petroleum Reserve stores oil reserves, DARPA helps companies innovate, and NEST prevents nuclear reactor and refinery meltdowns.

Department of Defense (730,000 members)

New DOD is the USAF, USN, USMC, USA, and CBP. Our air force, army and navy have secretaries. Coast guard and border patrol reports to a commissioner. CIA hires a director. Defense ministers and their three secretaries double as Joint Chiefs of Staff! U.S. president is the only person capable of authorizing nuclear launches. CIA renders DIA, ROA and NGA obsolete and provides the military all its satellite photography. USSF is reorganized as the U.S. Space Legion, manning USAF's STRATCOM, our own nuclear defense grid! Sell all but 150 military satellites to reputable allied nations.

Scrap all existing inventory within aircraft boneyards, vehicular junkyards and mothball fleets. From now on, each branch only maintains one of these bases at once. Continuously scrap older husks to cannibalize parts for our current assets.

Department of Justice (100,000 members)

Bureau of Enforcement: (20,000 members)

U.S. attorney general is head over the Dept. of Justice. FBI investigates and DEA tackles illicit drug distribution. ATF issues permits for distilleries, guns and firearms. Our correctional system runs prisons and jails. Correctional officers (COs) lead chain gangs through the wilderness to collect seeds, moss and fungal spores for rangers.

Bureau of Enterprise: (20,000 members)

Inspector General monitors government waste. Once ignored, they whistle-blow to gain attention from citizens. Roll the copyright, patent, trademark and registration offices into one group. FTC protects citizens against identity theft. OSHA stands up for our wage slaves. FCC targets false advertisement instead of enforcing censorship.

Bureau of Health Services: (40,000 members)

Surgeon general is a retired military general officer who leads the PHS. FDA tests products before issuing them nutrition labels. USDA inspects farm goods and offers food stamps (SNAP) to the truly needy. FEMA mitigates potential biological disasters.

Bureau of Education: (20,000 members)

Privatize all U.S. education! My Academic Administration regulates public school districts, private academic guilds and university systems. Scholarship Administration awards grants to worthy candidates. Nutrition Administration gives underprivileged kids meal benefits and Child Protective Services (CPS) assists in child abuse programs.

Department of Treasury (160,000 members)

Treasury secretary leads entire department while treasurers oversee minting. USDT includes the U.S. Treasury, U.S. Mint, Federal Reserve, FDIC (banks), FCUA (credit unions), SIPC (brokerages) and IRS. Fed is a central bank with a public-private model.

Elucidation

Executive cabinets maintain four departments and one press secretary. Defense ministers report directly to the U.S. president. Chiefs of staff serve as gatekeepers between their secretary of state, secretary of treasury and U.S. attorney general.

Administrators run administrations, commissioners lead bureaus, treasurers help maintain treasuries and secretaries command the service branches within our military.

State and local governments utilize similar cabinet models with press secretaries. Departments focus on education, enforcement, public infrastructure and parks.

Tribal Parties

Eagle Federation

This temporary group disbands after Operation White Wolf is completed. Afterwards, run open parties with two, four-year term limits. The White House is a great house serving as our country's presidential palace. It maintains a large retinue of formal servants. Governors' mansions are stately homes and charge visitors for public tours!

U.S. President: Head of state decrees executive orders and condition of the Union.

Vice-president: Head of U.S. Congress. Leads senate, breaks ties and serves as VP.

Speaker: Leads U.S. Council of Representatives. Maintains order and breaks ties.

Pro tempore: Both houses can appoint an ad hoc substitute in one's absence.

Chamberlain: Chief federal justice overturns laws, leads tribunals and impeaches.

Judicial Leagues

Eight regional sprachbunds create their own leagues divided into parties. Internal wings run primaries against one another to enroll future federal justice candidates. Amendments can ensure U.S. presidents must elect these individuals to tighten the qualifications of these individuals regardless of the POTUS's political alignment. Federal and state justices work on court tribunals to review bills' constitutionality.

Peacemakers: Chairmen (Unisex Titles)

Peacekeepers: Trustees (Board Members)

First Nations

Historically, each of the lower 48's contiguous states were dominated by one first nation. They'll enroll candidates for state governor, senator and justice. Judges are elected. Within the Senate, fold 100 senators into 22 standing committees, each led by chairmen who speak directly to the VP. Puerto Rico becomes a state with open parties, one governor and two U.S. senators. Hawaii transforms itself into a duchy state with their monarch's royal family dwelling in a palace rated as a stately house. Voters elect two U.S. senators. State senates now fold into 12 standing committees tasked with reassembling proposed house bills attempting to pass new legislation.

Dreamweavers: Chairmen (Unisex Titles)

Windtalkers: Trustees (Board Members)

State Directory

1. **Alabama:** Alabama
2. **Arizona:** Navajo
3. **Arkansas:** Caddo
4. **California:** Yurok
5. **Colorado:** Lakota
6. **Connecticut:** Mohegan
7. **Delaware:** Munsee
8. **Florida:** Seminole
9. **Georgia:** Muscogee
10. **Idaho:** Nez Perce
11. **Illinois:** Illinois
12. **Indiana:** Miami
13. **Iowa:** Ioway
14. **Kansas:** Kaw
15. **Kentucky:** Shawnee
16. **Louisiana:** Coushatta
17. **Maine:** Penobscot
18. **Maryland:** Piscataway
19. **Massachusetts:** Massachusett
20. **Michigan:** Chippewa
21. **Minnesota:** Menominee
22. **Mississippi:** Choctaw
23. **Missouri:** Missouria
24. **Montana:** Blackfeet
25. **Nebraska:** Pawnee
26. **Nevada:** Shoshone
27. **New Hampshire:** Pennacook
28. **New Jersey:** Lenape
29. **New Mexico:** Apache
30. **New York:** Seneca
31. **North Carolina:** Lumbee
32. **North Dakota:** Dakota
33. **Ohio:** Huron
34. **Oklahoma:** Wichita
35. **Oregon:** Coquille
36. **Pennsylvania:** Susquehannock
37. **Rhode Island:** Niantic
38. **South Carolina:** Catawba
39. **South Dakota:** Sioux
40. **Tennessee:** Cherokee
41. **Texas:** Commanche
42. **Utah:** Ute
43. **Vermont:** Abenaki
44. **Virginia:** Patowomec
45. **Washington:** Yakama
46. **West Virginia:** Tutelo
47. **Wisconsin:** Winnebago
48. **Wyoming:** Arapaho

Hawaii

Royal Family:

Monarchs are called dukes (males) or duchesses (female). Address rulers as, "Your highness." Child leaders in nonage add infante before their titles while prime ministers serve as regents until they mature. Since Hawaii isn't a separate country, don't call them grand dukes. Archdukes were Austria's way of trying to one-up everyone else. The latter sounded way better. Spouses become royal consorts only after marriage.

Honor Guard:

During war, the POTUS assumes direct command over Hawaii's National Guard and auxiliary forces. However, part of their Army National Guard serves as royal guards. Moreover, they stay behind as permanent detachments occupying the state palace. Those soldiers carry ceremonial M14s outfitted with 7.62mm rounds and bayonets.

Executive Cabinet:

Alongside parliamentary support, heads of state also appoint new prime ministers. Premiers begin filling cabinet ministry positions working at the pleasure of their ruler. Ineffective legislatures can be dissolved forcing new elections within said parliaments. Unlike diets, monarchs can dismiss the upper house's lords and exercise reserve powers to block unconstitutional laws. Actions require advice by their prime ministers.

Parliament

House of Commons:

Premiers are selected by the Hawaiian House of Commons and must maintain majority support to remain in control. Unsatisfactory cabinets might receive censure towards one or more ministers. Motions of no-confidence target all members of parliament (MPs). House speakers maintain order and break ties. There shall be a total of 51 MPs.

House of Lords:

Monarchs award chivalrous subjects their historic noble and ignoble titles once held by Hawaiian tribes. Nobility can run for office and hold peerage in the upper house. Unlike other MPs, lords lack term limits. A second speaker also breaks ties too! Limit them to 25 MPs. Doing so helps both houses transition without changing their size.

High Court

For supreme courts, rulers appoint justices to lifetime positions and can easily depose them. Judges are elected directly by voters. Ideally, only candidates with previous experience as legal attorneys should qualify for selection in either circumstance. Not every state enforces these guidelines, but I strongly recommend they acquire them.

Greater Tribes

Federal Districts: 484 Provinces

Establish one tribe per greater city area. Wings select federal representatives, county justices and local candidates. Elect 484 U.S. councilors who fold into 22 standing committees. Their chairmen communicate directly to the lower house's speaker. Boards are further divided into two select subcommittees, each led by vice-chairmen.

Paramounts: Chairmen (Unisex Titles)

Chiefs: Trustees (Board Members)

County Bands: 1,194 Prefectures

Tribes split into bands responsible for controlling individual counties. Wings enroll justice and court constable candidates. Two-thirds of pre-existing ghost counties become "ranges" inside the new U.S. National Park System, governed by our state rangers. Ghost towns are repurposed as living quarters for park rangers and deputies.

Principals: Chairmen (Unisex Titles)

Chieftains: Trustees (Board Members)

Local Clans: 6,112 Incorporations

Bands further divide into clans, not to be confused with family associations. The latter are organizations backing family-owned businesses and nonprofit charities, groups helping them avoid discrimination lawsuits from non-natives. They appoint town candidates. Elect four councilors and one mayor. City outskirts are called parishes. The outer portions of townships subdivide into four shires (farming neighborhoods).

Chiefs: Chairmen (Unisex Titles)

Elders: Trustees (Board Members)

Communities

Zoning and Restrictions:

Local governments quarter land uses. Deed restrictions force subdivisions, condos and apartments to be gated HOA communities. Relocate POAs to business districts and establish chambers of commerce (COCs) in city divisions. Towns have four village communities superintended by chairmen. Hamlet neighborhoods are led by trustees.

Tribal Positions:

Firekeepers: Vice-chairmen act as speakers during a chairman's absence.

Potlatches: Treasurers grant equal funding to primaries and candidates.

Warriors: Whips control the wings and select candidates for their party.

Order 66

Big Brother (*1984*):

Residential communities seek freedom from tyrannical POAs, security patrols placing residents under the microscope for loitering at public amenities and surveillance cameras invading residents' privacy. Upscale neighborhoods desiring security forces should limit details to 2-5 members split across shifts. Duties should be restricted to manning guard shacks and responding to important service calls without partiality.

Vigilante Injustice:

As for neighborhood watches, people need to mind their own damn business! More attention should be focused on preventing predators from preying on little children. Otherwise, embrace the Second Amendment, study karate and lift weights! Let street fights settle duels! Citizen's arrests allow the public to beat the crap out of someone and detain them. Actual arrests are performed by cops. According to my plan, CPS commends parents for whipping little kids, especially daughters, into submission!

Execution

86'd Dead Plates:

Businesses suffer from the opposite dilemma. CCTV cameras in some culinary establishments only record up to 30 minutes of footage and have blind spots. Additionally, security guards are crucial to many businesses. Whoever can't afford bouncers should carry guns. Bounty hunters eliminate the need for undercover stings. Therefore, law enforcement prioritizes defending government-held property.

Medicine Men:

Spiritual healers aren't part of political parties and fall under the private sector. Born-again, Native American men and women are hand-picked by God to perform his miracles on others. Read *The Early Church* for more information on this subject. Sabbatarian Gentiles and Messianic Jews believing in tithing 10% are candidates.

CHAPTER THREE

Governing Branches

Quadrant 1:2

Listed below is this chapter's section directory. Topics are grouped together in subsections labeled by underlined bullets. Any further subdivision of information is organized into verses marked by bolded bullets.

Overview

Leadership

Freedom of Choice:

White Wolf specified which of its future national governments are constitutional monarchies or republics. Each tribal civilization has its own unique culture. To further their advancements, every possible governmental model detailing representative democracy has been included! Certain options could benefit them more than others.

Capital Districts:

National and provincial counties called capital districts contain everyone's capital cities. Normally, most also house the seats of government drafting new legislation. Sometimes, countries' capitol buildings can be found in entirely different prefectures.

Military Defense:

Additionally, which capitol is selected determines what kind of military organization is at their disposal. Some might have neutral military branches, others only national police agencies. Quadrant III reveals how to properly organize these defense forces.

Diplomatic Relations:

The following sections discuss what type of heads of state or government future diplomats will find themselves addressing. Therefore, it's imperative they read this chapter beforehand. Otherwise, it'll hinder establishing any new ambassadorships!

Liberties

We the People:

Ignorance leads to class warfare and useful idiots manipulated by underground cabals plotting treason against loyal citizens. Too many people desire surrendering more emergency power to potential candidates in exchange for not having to learn or assume accountability for their own life's responsibilities. Upon doing so, these freedoms are forever forfeited. Stupidity is choosing the wrong answer on purpose.

U.S. Government

Legislatures

Local Prefectures:

Local government encompasses townships and municipalities. Town mayors are heads of government voting in councils and directly managing cabinets. Major cities limit executive powers and give them to city managers. Minor anchors hybridize both concepts by letting mayors retain full authority after appointing cabinet managers. Unlike local unicameral (single-house) incorporations, all state capitols are bicameral (dual-house). Councilors represent voting districts and senators major state regions.

State Provinces:

Select subcommittees listen to special interest groups, aka lobbyists. These think tanks funnel into standing committees proposing new bills. Speakers maintain order and break ties. Bills funnel upwards towards state senates. Senators lack subcommittees. Lieutenant governors will maintain order and break ties within the upper chambers.

Federal Government:

Presidents and vice-presidents replace governors and lieutenant governors at federal levels. Both executives share two things in common: First, heads of state can sign or veto new laws. Also, a $2/3^{rds}$ overrule can overturn said decision into effect. Congress declares war, ratifies treaties, awards certain military medals and sets annual budgets. Councilors vote to impeach officials forcing their senates to conduct trials.

Cabinets

State Governors:

Governors double as heads of government with the capacity to vote or veto law proposed by state capitols. Heads of state lead cabinets and are allowed two, four-year term limits. During peace, they lead state militias. For clemency, reprieves can postpone executions, commutations reduce court sentences and pardons exonerate. U.S. presidents issue pardons to individuals and amnesty to groups or organizations.

U.S. Presidents:

Proposals must be signed, pocket vetoed by ignoring documents for 10 days, or outright vetoed. Executive orders further clarify congressional laws to any existing cabinet members. Annual State of the Union Addresses give Congress situational awareness. A POTUS's diplomacy efforts open the door for future ambassadors.

Judiciaries

County Prefectures:

Local incorporations lack their own judicial branch because they share a county courthouse. My city's police, town's sheriff's department and jails are all considered executive in nature. So, split them up into smaller, localized organizations instead of large, countywide organizations! Constabulary forces are judiciary police tasked with safeguarding public locations like tax offices, title record buildings and county fairs.

Statutory Courts:

A county's justice, court constable and judges are elected directly by voters. Judges should be qualified legal attorneys. Some states' constitutions don't require them to have these qualifications. Term lengths differ according to state law. Tribunals are held to interpret local legislation and can deem ridiculous laws as unconstitutional.

Supreme Courts:

Each state has its own constitution determining how nominations will be held. As of 2024, Oregon and Texas allow citizens to vote for their candidates. Everyone else relies on governors to appoint future members to lifetime terms. Court cases focus primarily on appeals proving if the previous verdicts given were constitutional or not.

Extenuations

Commanders-in-Chief:

During war, Hawaii always retains its honor guard armed with ceremonial M14s. During WWII, two U.S. deputy CNCs were commissioned: General Marshall and Fleet Admiral King, who led their respective service branches. However, my plan abolishes four-star, five-star and six-star ranks by selecting top-retired officers as future aides, adjutants, branch secretaries and defense ministers who can lead formations into battle. Additionally, allied heads of government shall now command these theaters!

Nuclear Warfare:

Existing nuclear treaties must be amended to allow nuclear ABM testing. Otherwise, we won't be able to convert our ICBMs into anti-ballistic missiles (ABMs) without breaking contract. DEFCON-1 status requires immediate action to counter incoming nuclear strikes. Martial law can be declared during crises by presidents and governors on state levels. These actions, along with their curfews, must be limited in duration.

Emergency Powers:

Normally, vice-presidents are nothing more than the president of the senate. Yet, they can also serve as interim heads of state, heads of government and deputy CNCs whenever a POTUS finds themselves incapacitated for extended periods of time (coma, surgery, etc.) or go missing. VPs are succeeded by house speakers if need be.

Separation of Powers

Dualism

Federated Republic:

Federations are home to provinces called states. Governors can resist unfair laws and decrees forced on them by federal governments. Russian states are dubbed republics led by presidents. One union of states creates a single federated nation. Monarchies in the form of kingdoms and commonwealths often house states. For example: Japan.

Assembly-independent:

As of 2024, only three independent bodies exist. Switzerland is a directorial system, discussed in the following section. Micronesian and Surinamese presidents get elected by legislatures, not voters. Parliaments need chancellors as their premiers, which is discussed in the next section. Paralleling the UK's Commonwealth, four more shall be formed according to White Wolf, three led by an assembly-independent republic! Moreover, presidents within member states are elected directly by voters.

Houses

Multicameralism:

Unicameralism accommodates small countries and local government. Bicameralism balances representation between voting districts and regions of state provinces. As historic racial tensions and social castes ended, tetracameralism did too. Afterwards, tricameralism was rendered obsolete after standing committees were introduced. Lower houses dwarf upper chambers twofold and require numerous subcommittees.

Congressional Republic:

Rome inspired most of the republican capitols we see today. Plebian councils and patrician-led senates weren't truly bicameral because they could pass bills without support from both houses. While monarchies dissolved parliaments, presidential systems couldn't remove lawmakers from exercising floor control. Checks and balances bestowed all three branches strength to resist unconstitutional legislation.

Semi-parliamentary:

Israel was the last to experiment with this model. Unlike full parliaments, prime ministers were elected directly by the public! Almost everything else conducted within semi-parliaments fused power across branches, but this is one example of separation of powers. Few republican capitols ever offered this to their citizens.

Interims

Pro Tempore:

House leaders, regardless of chamber, appoint pro tempores to substitute in one's absence. Different countries might employ their own unique titles, but they're all essentially pro tempores. Heirs to an official elected position are called incumbents.

De jure Resistance:

Rightful heirs lay claim to something. Constitutional monarchies grant their monarchs reserve powers letting them hold power as de jure leaders. Counter-revolutionaries dubbed as freedom fighters differ from insurgents attempting to stage a coup d'état. The former are often designated as loyalist nationalists and latter separatist rebels.

Military Juntas:

As empires fell, socialist regimes overtook everything outside the Western Bloc. We had to cooperate with Stalin's communists during WWII and pit one military junta against another throughout the Cold War. Pick your battles; let's divide and conquer!

De facto Regimes:

Dictatorships center around one-party rule. There are key differences between China and North Korea. Chinese chairmen require party support to remain in power while North Korean supreme leaders cannot be trumped by anyone under them. Absolute monarchies remain legitimate because most subjects remain satisfied and at peace.

Civil Rights

Religious Freedom:

Roger Williams referenced the metaphorical 'high wall' preventing governments from committing religious persecution through theocratic rule. This is separation of church and state. Nonprofit organizations, public or not, are charities. Early 21st century churches only give 3% of funds to poor members and most don't even tithe 10%. Stronger tax laws need to be proposed to promote legitimacy and transparency.

Presidential Elections:

Heads of state cannot create family dynasties. All politicians have term limits, which can be different in certain countries or states. Assemblies-independent appoint and depose presidencies while congresses let their citizens elect all potential candidates.

Checks and Balances:

Absolute monarchs cannot be held accountable to their own subjects' constitution. Westminster lawmakers hold sovereignty elevating them above the law. There are plenty of reasons why these politicians must hold these rights within their systems of government, but it's why most American people prefer our separation of powers.

Fusion of Powers

Executive

Semi-constitutional:

Constitutions offer a degree of democracy to subjects by allowing legislatures, courts and prefectures executive branches. Unitary governments cannot challenge national decrees. Monarchs wield full executive authority over their country's cabinets. A prime minister acts as the head of government, but rulers can fight unfair laws by exercising reserve powers. Doing so often requires counseling from PMs and advisors.

Semi-presidential:

Premier-presidential systems differ since cabinets report directly to the legislatures. Heads of state still serve as commanders-in-chief over armed forces and can dissolve parliaments forcing new elections. President-parliamentary models grant rulers authority over executive cabinets and the ability to appoint prime ministers upon obtaining majority support amongst lawmakers. Reserve powers permit them to refuse accepting unjust bills, but are limited compared to our congressional version.

Non-executive

Ceremonial Diet:

Throughout history, heads of state in diets lacked the ability to dissolve unicameral governments or the upper houses in bicameral models. Legally, cabinet advisors must be consulted beforehand. No reserve powers are given to influence bills or cabinet decisions. Instead of premiers, chancellors head government wielding greater power.

Sovereign Parliament:

Legislative supremacy exempts law makers from being held accountable by their own constitution. No high court or executive cabinet could provide them a series of checks and balances. Monarchs wielded great influence over cabinets, court appointments and upper houses. To combat this, the Westminster system elevated its lower house over all else! Countries under parliamentary sovereignties double as unitary states.

Directorial System:

Switzerland's federation still refers to itself as a confederacy. Citizens participate in direct democracy by voting on every issue at any level! The lower house represents people while an upper chamber focuses on counties. A seven-person federal council serves as its head of state. Cabinet ministers take turns as the presiding officers!

Review

Marriage

Divorce Courts:

Upon earning her husband's trust, Queen Esther was promised up to half of King Ahasuerus's estate. Yet, nowhere in the Bible does it state all other divorcees are obligated to half their spouse's assets! Countless estranged parents witnessed offspring brainwashed against them, visitation rights stripped away and alimony bleed them dry. Men suffered the most, but many breadwinning wives fell victim too.

Prenuptial Agreements:

Besides prenups, I recommend U.S. couples protect their assets by filing private LLCs and separate bank accounts. Breadwinners can give allowances to their spouses in a joint checking account. Flee from the thought of co-ownership on property titles. Marriages by the church don't require state licenses, therefore protecting spouses.

Child Support Caps:

Annuities should be limited to no more than $12,000 USD FY2024. Anyone incapable of sustaining this due to financial constraints can negotiate up to 20% of one's annual income. New CD laws grant children a monthly allowance towards daily meals on a debit card. The remaining principal remains untouched until they reach maturity.

Mitigation

Corporal Punishment:

Deadly attacks on feeble elders, the retarded, lame, wounded and little children still fall under battery. However, citizens duke it out until one is in submission! Women can be slapped and youth spanked for disrespect in public regardless of one's gender!

Infringement Laws:

First Amendment rights can only go so far. Laws against bearing false witness in the form of slander, false advertisement and copywrite infringement are strictly enforced.

CHAPTER FOUR

Gold Silver Standard

<u>Quadrant 1:3</u>

Listed below is this chapter's section directory. Topics are grouped together in subsections labeled by underlined bullets. Any further subdivision of information is organized into verses marked by bolded bullets.

Overview

Exchange

Hybrid Theory:

During 1775, Continental dollars were worth $40.79 FY2024. To reduce currency devaluation without destabilizing the economy, eliminate outdated fiat models. Combine $1b in coinage, $60bil of treasury stock and $18t as electronic money! Most of our cash resides overseas and in vaults, safes or homes creating hyperinflation compared to our founding years, yet cashiers regularly experience coin shortages.

Treasury Stock:

National stock looks exactly like bills, but aren't promissory notes issued by banks. They're small denomination certificates spending most of their time in bank vaults backing our historic reserve percentages. Therefore, currency inflation isn't affected!

National Assets:

As of 2024, the U.S. population exceeded 340 million holding $269t in assets. There's a way to replace them with 120 million people without dropping values below $180t. Skilled, blue-collar jobs generate more revenue than most non-essential, pink-collar services. Many extort customers in to paying unfair tip percentages for subpar labor.

Savings

Self-directed IRAs:

Reserves are sold to precious metal dealers in the form of 911 bars. IRA custodians market retirees tangible bouillon. Self-employed individuals open self-directed IRAs. A single account can simultaneously hold different kinds of precious metals at once.

Bank Reserves:

Retirement investments and bank reserves are stored within insured bank vaults. Reinforce historic percentages of minimum reserves in financial institutions to 10% within communities, 20% in regional branches and 25% along the national level.

Minted Coinage

*Cast satin coins generate musicality during ping tests. Graphene alloys prevent fine silver from scratching, denting, shaving, being clipped or melting. Chemical coatings prevent tarnish. Registers house seven coin slots and five rows of rolls.

Cent Pieces

$0.01: Full "Penny"

Bronze pennies always contain 0.375g fine silver and 2.625g of 80/20 yellow bronze. Obverses broadcast Chief Pontiac's bust. Shield murals atop rears resemble Lincoln's Memorial. Reverse cameo rears and deep cameo on edges. (Value is $0.40 FY2024) FYI: Britian introduced the ha' penny during the 13th century worth over $10 today! Population growth drove silver values up to the point where they had to inflate their currency to account for pettier purchases and mint enough coinage into circulation.

$0.02: Full "Pence"

Pence pieces combine 0.75g fine silver and 3.25g of 80/20 yellow bronze. Faces show an image of Geronimo. Rear murals have small moto shields found on old coinage. Apply reverse cameo on rears and deep cameo along edges. (Value is $0.80 FY2024)

$0.05: The "Nickel"

Nickel-silver alloys mix 1.5g fine silver with 3.5g nickel. Obverse facades display an image of Chief Tecumseh while their rears showcase an American timber bison. Layer reverse cameo atop rear murals and deep cameo over ridges. (Value is $2.00 FY2024)

$0.10: The "Dime"

Dimes were never bigger weighing in at 3g fine silver! Chief Blackhawk adorns obverse facades while tail murals incorporate an olive branch, flaming torch and oak branch. Install reverse cameo tail images and deep cameo knife ridges. (Value is $4.00 FY2024)

$0.25: "Quarter-dollar"

Quarter dollars get 6g in fine silver. Chief Sitting Bull heads and eagle mural as tails. Run reverse cameo on tail murals and deep cameo on knife ridges. (Value is $10.00 in FY2024)

$0.50: *"Half-dollar"*

Half dollars must be allocated 12g in fine silver. Chief Crazy Horse heads and Department of Defense (DOD) Seal aboard tails. Reverse cameo tail murals and deep cameo knife ridges. (Value is $20.00 FY2024) Popular amongst sporting and gambling organizations!

$1.00: Silver "Dollar"

Quarter dollars grant holders up to 24g fine silver. Sacagawea heads and Great Seal mural tails. Reverse cameo murals and deep cameo knife ridges. (Value is $40.00 in FY2024)

Treasury Stock

*Series 1928 Greenbacks consist of recycled denim scraps. Stock certificates are 25% linen and 75% cotton. Sprinkling cast 80/20 yellow bronze over them creates a trinity of awards: Silver coinage, gold bullion and bronze stock certificates!

Certificates

$2.00: "Queer" Dollar

Faces combine 1928 fronts with John Jay's bust. This man was our first chief justice; a superior alternative to Thomas Jefferson, who forced many Eastern tribes off their land! For rears, apply borders from Trumbull's *Declaration of Independence* around murals off old $1.00 bills. Replace the Eye of Providence with an image of Lady Liberty and trade the U.S. Great Seals for our Liberty Bell! (Value is $80.00 FY2024)

$5.00: "Five" Bucks

Faces combine the front of 1928 queer bills with John Marshall's bust. He was our longest-serving chief justice. Lincoln approved the largest execution in American history and forced Indian relocation further west! Remodeled 1928 backs trade Lincoln's Memorial for mural of the U.S. Supreme Court. (Value is $200.00 FY2024)

$10.00: "Ten" Bucks

Alexander Hamilton 1963 faces and 1928 *Car & Treasury* on rears. He's the founder of our national treasury system! Hamilton College was originally a school for Native Americans before it degraded into a liberal arts institution! (Value is $400.00 FY2024)

$20.00: "Twenty" Bucks

James Madison's bust inside '95 faces and '28 *White House* rears. Cited as the Father of the U.S. Constitution. Jackson initiated the Trail of Tears. Moreover, he was brutal towards his slaves. Accounts of him attempting to stop a slave from getting whipped, including artwork depicting the event, are falsified events! (Value is $800.00 FY2024)

$50.00: "Fifty" Bucks

John Hancock's bust inside '63 faces with '29 *U.S. Capitol* rears. This founding father was the famous VP inspiring, "Give me your Hancock!" (Value is $2,000.00 FY2024)

$100.00: The "Benjamin"

Benjamin Franklin faces and *Independence Hall* backs. Combine pre-1990 fronts with post-1990 rear border trim. Keep current 2013 model's building. Few citizens realize Ben Franklin was also a congressman. Continental Congress met in Independence Hall, which signed the Declaration of Independence long before Capitol Hill existed.

911 Bullion Bars

Contributions

Troy Oz.: 20 dwt.

John Paul Jones over faces and Declaration of Independence onto rears. Rear Admiral Jones is the Father of the American Navy. He served under Commodore Esek Hopkins during the Revolutionary War before quickly surpassing him in action by character. Rear murals are the presentations of John Trumbull's *Declaration of Independence*. This painting replaced the Jefferson Memorial as the rear mural used on $2.00 bills.

Troy Lb.: 12 oz. (t)

General Grant along faces and Surrendered General rears. Ulysses S. Grant was the third person to be promoted posthumously to the rank of General of the Armies in 2022, itself a six-star rank. He led the Union Army during the American Civil War and mentored General Sherman, the latter famous for his scorched earth polices. He was the 18th president. Rear murals present Trumbull's *Surrender of General Burgoyne*.

Ton Bar: 100 oz. (t)

Admiral Dewey adorns faces and de Soto's Discovery compliments rears. George Dewey was promoted to Admiral of the Navy; an honorary, six-star rank created just for him. His squadron defeated the Spanish Armada at the Battle of Manila Bay. He singlehandedly ended the Spanish-American War while only losing one sailor! Rear murals display Frederick Girsch's *de Soto discovering the Mississippi*. The word ton is also British slang for 100. Anything this valuable belongs in our national bank vaults.

Good Delivery: 400 oz. (t)

General Pershing along faces and Washington's Resignation rears. John. J. Pershing was awarded the title General of the Armies, a six-star rank. He led the American Expeditionary Force (AEF) during the Battle of Argonne Forest, which ended the Great War! He was nicknamed Blackjack because he was famous for incorporating African American units. Rear murals showcase Frederick Girsch's *Washington resigning his commission*. State central banking stockpiles most of our nation's good delivery bars.

Kilobar: 1,000 oz. (t)

Place Admiral Leahy upon faces and Embarking Pilgrims on rears. William D. Leahy was a fleet admiral who served as chairman to the Joint Chiefs of Staff during WWII, a post held only by our country's most senior servicemen. He was a retired admiral who provided advice to the war secretary. Rear murals depict Robert Walter Weir's *Embarking of the Pilgrims*. Federal Reserve stores most of these golden kilobars.

Review

Securities

Public Exchange:

Don't confuse treasury stock with treasuries! Most minted stock certificates spend their time backing historic percentages in bank vaults. Contractors lack card readers and don't like paying merchant fees. They're paid several times a day and can't make repeated trips to banks. Personal checks cover capital expenditures. Treasuries differ by being investments bearing interest to their account holders. Government bills, notes and bonds finance future projects and reduce deficits combating existing debt.

U.S. Treasuries:

T-bills: Most checking and savings accounts earn interest because of T-bills.

T-notes: Fuels money market (bank version), mutual fund and CD accounts.

T-bonds: Powers a bank's savings bonds, trust funds and retirement accounts.

Government Bonds:

Municipal: Prevents deficits during renovation projects to public infrastructure.

War: Always issue Series EE regardless of how small your future conflicts are.

Savings: Emergency use only. Once debt clocks are paid, stop printing them!

Investments

U.S. Money Supply:

M0: Narrow Money. Cash comes in the form of coinage and treasury stock.

MB: Monetary Base. Cash plus reserves. Crypto is an MM (money multiplier).

M1: Near Money. Checking (MZM is zero maturity), savings and cash accounts.

M2: Broad Money. Defined as money markets, mutual funds and CD accounts.

M3: Bond Money. Bank savings bonds, trust funds and retirement accounts.

M4: Far Money. Corporate paper (IOUs are M4-) and government securities.

(L): Banker's Acceptance. BAs issued by banks serve as IOUs to creditors.

CHAPTER FIVE

Public Infrastructure

<u>Quadrant 1:4</u>

Listed below is this chapter's section directory. Topics are grouped together in subsections and verses mark any further subdivision of information.

Overview

Rebellion

No Man's Land:

We must take control of as much real estate as possible. Otherwise, even more waves of non-native immigrants could flood into whatever footholds your people are trying to establish. My plan shifts population patterns between cities and towns to 55/45. Doing so gives towns more of a voice politically and makes future generations more conservative. Enacting zoning laws in rural outskirts restricts their overdevelopment.

Green Conspiracy:

Alaskan rivers shown are releasing heavy metals in regions without heavy industry. The only way this is possible would be if leftists sabotaged them to prove Global Warming is real. Ironically, SE Texas experienced the coldest winters on record and isn't normally supposed to get snow. It's all part of a plan to brainwash useful idiots into supporting their efforts to shut down American industry. Thus, crippling us enough so our enemies can topple our country forever. Let's prove them wrong! Encourage heavy industry to be greener and lower emissions through tax deductions.

Resistance

Master Planning:

Most of local debt is attributed by a lack of master planning and municipal bonds. A smaller handful of taller buildings and two-way streets devour less land, maintain fewer roadways, experience less traffic and offer affordable public transportation. Walking cities and townships let smaller law enforcement agencies do a better job.

Urban Forestry:

Greenbelts can drop temperatures by 45°F! Plants reduce CO_2, increase oxygen and clean up air pollution too. Replacing concrete channels with bottomland forests prevents erosion, purifies water and controls mosquitos with carnivorous bulrush. Urban forests improve privacy while sound barriers reduce noise in subdivisions.

Combined Statistical Areas

Provinces

Greater Areas: 484 Anchors

<u>Megas</u>: 4 **(256,000 to 1,024,000 people)**

4 megalopolis municipalities x 1,024,000 people = 4,096,000 people

<u>Metros</u>: 80 **(64,000 to 256,000 people)**

80 metropolis municipalities x 256,000 people = 20,480,000 people

<u>Micros</u>: 200 **(16,000 to 64,000 people)**

200 micropolis municipalities 64,000 people = 12,800,000 people

<u>Satellites</u>: 200 **(8,000 to 16,000 people)**

200 "de facto" municipalities x 16,000 people = 3,200,000 people

Minor Anchors: 704 Micros

<u>Micros</u>: 704 **(16,000 to 32,000 people)**

704 micropolis municipalities x 32,000 people = 22,528,000 people

Prefectures

Counties: 1,194 Seats

Townships: 6,112 Incorporations

<u>Satellites</u>: 1,504 **(8,000 to 16,000 people)**

1,504 "5A district" satellite towns x 16,000 people = 24,064,000 people

<u>Markets</u>: 2,307 **(4,000 to 8,000 people)**

2,304 "4A district" market towns x 8,000 people = 18,432,000 people

<u>Commuters</u>: 2,307 **(2,000 to 4,000 people)**

2,304 "3A district" commuter towns x 4,000 people = 9,216,000 people

Residential Areas: 28,704 HOAs

<u>Community Size</u>: **(500 to 4,000 people)**

<u>Community Totals</u>: **(114,816,000 people)**

Greaters

Major Anchors:

Agglomerations are orbited by rings of rural counties filled with towns. These include megalopolitans (large), metropolitans (medium) and micropolitans (small). Some are too remote to have a city as its anchor. Therefore, certain satellite towns step up as "de facto" cities! Hubs surrounded by cities instead of townships are conurbations. Metroplexes have two or more major cites as anchors. A prime example is the Dallas-Fort Worth Metroplex. The largest of primate cities might be Alpha ++ global cities.

Statistical Areas:

Megalopolitan anchor cities are orbited by 16 micros, 16 satellites, 16 markets and 16 commuters. Surround metropolitans with eight micros, eight satellites, eight markets and eight commuters. Micropolitans require four satellites, four markets and four commuters. De facto cities have no satellites, four markets and four commuters.

Megalopolises: 400,000-acre municipalities, 80,000-acre cities.

Metropolises: 200,000-acre municipalities, 40,000-acre cities.

Micropolises: 100,000-acre municipalities, 20,000-acre cities.

Satellites: 40,000-acre civil townships, 8,000-acre towns.

Markets: 20,000-acre civil townships, 4,000-acre towns.

Commuters: 10,000-acre civil townships, 2,000-acre towns.

Planning

Municipalities:

Walking cities require much less land. Place 2/3rds of it in future state park systems. Parkway loops connect all minor anchors together. The remaining 1/3rd forms its municipality, itself split 80/20 between parish outskirts and proper city limits. Parish farmland is orbited by greenways and linked to towns by FM roads. Beltways border the actual city limits. For civil townships, farms lie farm beyond their towns' loops.

Administrations:

Divide megalopolises into four boroughs (16 divisions), metropolises four divisions (16 districts) and micropolises four districts. Divisionary chambers of commerce and district POAs prevent city councils from exceeding five members include the mayor.

City Propers:

Uptown suburbs give way to midtown tenements as one delves deeper intown. Upon reaching downtown, suburban boulevards become avenues. Alleys provide access to parking garages. Boxed within four avenues lies a city plaza's central roundabout.

Real Estate Development

Downtowns

Urban Centers:

Bronze musical fountains double as memorials encircled by flowerbeds. Calcada sett promenades lead pedestrians away from them through grass courtyards. Green signs explain dog rules. Mosaic tile esplanades lined with trees separate these central yards from the 5-lane roundabouts. Orbiting the circular street are government buildings.

Town Centers:

Deep wells supply towers, which distribute water through aqueducts complemented by flowerbeds. Options include standpipes hidden inside clocktowers (commuters), multi-legs (markets) and hydropillars (satellites). Cobblestone promenades guide visitors back to their grass courtyards. Brick esplanades plant trees to shade benches.

City Skylines:

A smaller handful of taller skyscrapers and two-way streets is superior to vast swaths of shorter high-rises and one-way navigation. Set canopies to 45 stories inside megas, 30 within metros and 20 in micros. Emergent examples shouldn't exceed 2.5x this floor count. Dubai's skyline has an odd appearance because most of the buildings accompanying the Burj Khalifa aren't tall enough to achieve a properly-balanced look.

Zoning

Land Quartering:

Local incorporations, city or town, quarter land usage so only 1/4th is residential. This helps reduce their overall population and maximizes wooded greenbelts everywhere. Underpasses cradle understory bushes, interchanges subcanopy shrubs and canopy trees elsewhere. Residential greenbelts are mixed hardwood forests incorporating pine emergent and bushes along 2-3 sides of all houses, amenities and perimeters.

Midtown Projects:

Tenants are housed in tower blocks. Megas get 18 stories, metros 12 and micros eight. Underclass rent apartments and working-class opt for condominiums. For flats, square footage options vary from 400 (studio), 600 (one-bedroom), 800 (two-bedroom) and 1,000 (three-bedroom). Condo units offer 600 (single-bedroom), 800 (two-bedroom) and 1,000 (three-bedroom). Parking garages, public amenities and common grounds represent the PJs' other three sections of quartered land usage.

Restrictions

Uptown Subdivisions:

Groundscraper mid-rises in subsections grant megas six-stories with $1/24^{th}$ an acre per lot. Metros rank in at five floors with houses grabbing $1/12^{th}$. Micros nab four while homes enjoy $1/6^{th}$. Multiplexes sell lower-middle class townhomes 1,000 (two-bedroom), 1,500 (three-bedroom) and 2,000 (four-bedroom) sq. ft. options. Upscale villas cut megas $1/20^{th}$, metros $1/10^{th}$ and micros $1/5^{th}$. Quadplexes market future upper-middle class families 1,000 (two-bed), 1,500 (three-bed) and 2,000 (four-bed).

Mixed-income Housing:

Towns construct mixed-income villages and their garden-style low-rises are always three-story buildings. For lots, coaches run $1/16^{th}$ of an acre, carriages $1/8^{th}$, cabins $1/4^{th}$ and cottages ½. Underclass triplexes market coaches as 600 (single-bedroom), 800 (two-bed) and 1,000 (three-bed) sq. ft. options. Working class duplexes solicit 600 (single-bed), 800 (two-bed) and 1,000 (three-bed) sq. ft. selections to customers.

Single-family Detached:

Lower-middle class families pick between a 1,000 (two-bedroom), 1,500 (three-bedroom) and 2,000 (four-bedroom) cabin. Upper-middle classmen opt for 1,000 (two-bed), 1,500 (three-bed) and 2,000 (four-bed) cottages. Make them two stories!

Estates

Rural Homesteads:

Industrial parks allow permits for indoor growing operations between five, ten and 20 acres. Minimum plot sizes towards parish farmland demand 50 acres (megas), 100 (metros) and 200 (micros). Townships push 500 (satellites), 1,000 (markets) and 2,000 (commuters). Cannabis/medicinal farmers can negotiate smaller allocations. As populations grow, towns reclassify themselves and divide acreage minimums in half. Owners of plots exceeding these totals can split them into plural deeds. Existing smallholdings lacking sufficient minimum acreage are protected by grandfathering.

Education

Academic Districts:

Megas can have up to 64 school districts. Metros could average 16 while micros cut four 5As. Satellites sustain one 5A consisting of five campuses: A nursery, elementary, middle, junior and high school. Market towns' 4As are comprised of four: Nursery, elementary, middle and high schools. Commuters' 3As get three: Elementary, middle and high schooling. If someone runs their own independent nursery, then you have a 1A. Small private schools might hit 2A: Primary and secondary school. Some top 6A!

Thoroughfare Grids

City Streets

Roundabouts: Partial-access

Composite requires reinforced concrete beds and thin membrane asphalt. Five, one-way lanes rotate counterclockwise. Name it MAIN ST. and establish 35 mph speed limits. Three-color, protected stoplights grant access to four connectors, which are two-lane, one-way alleys. They link to the box created by four avenues along their four corners, themselves doubling as intersections. Right turns on red are prohibited.

Avenues: Partial-access

Thin membrane composite. Four lanes on each side dedicated to left, straight-left, straight and straight-right lined with bollards. Central tree planter has spots for U-turns and intersections fork to prevent left-turns from slowing other drivers down. Example: 1st AVE. Speed limit is 45 mph. The fourth light bulb assists left-hand turns. NYC has much fatter, one-way versions in some areas. However, if we can reduce the population by encouraging others to move elsewhere, then you can change them.

Boulevards: Partial-access

Identical composites. Three lanes on each side allow for straight-left, straight and straight-right. Central tree planter has spots for U-turns and intersections fork to prevent left-turns from slowing down others. Example: RICHMOND BLVD. Speed limit is 55 mph. Whenever they intersect highways, arteries have four-bulbs and veins three-color protectors. Never allow two veins to go at once! Otherwise, vehicles turning left crash into others on the other side heading straight! Time three intervals.

Alamedas: Partial-access

Links gated communities to boulevards. Otta Seal composite. Two lanes on each side allow straight-left and straight-right. Central tree planter accommodates U-turns. Example: CHERRYHILL DR. Posted speed limit is 35mph. Place stop signs along exits.

Alleys: Open-access

Provides access to parking garages and neighborhood blocks. Otta Seal composite. One lane per side along a two-way. Example: 1st ST. (downtown); CANDY CANE LN. Speed limits are 25 mph. Exits need red and white yield signs on top of steel poles.

Courts: Open-access

Same composite on cul-de-sacs. Example: HARBOUR TOWN CT. Traffic is limited to 15 mph. Exits have yellow, diamond-shaped, caution signs warning outgoing traffic.

Town Roads

Spurs: Limited-access

Villages line inner perimeters of loops while farming homesteads dot outskirts. Chip seal asphalt. Give them two lanes on each side plus an open turning lane. Example: SPUR LOOP 105. Not all loops are perfect circles. Some might be a semi-circle or a crescent quarter. School zones diminish 55 mph speed limits to 35 mph whenever they're active. Give them two lanes on each side, an open turning lane and wide verges. Four, four-way intersections display red "stopper" blinkers along all sections.

Branches: Limited-access

Concurrencies lay thin membrane. Two lanes on each side plus one turning lane. These business routes require green shields. Example: BR 105 or 149. Cap speeds to 55mph. Once they merge into junctions, you'll see blinking, yellow "caution" lights warning about pedestrians. Each branch has a switch road to access rear parking lots.

Junctions: Limited-access

Town junctions broadcast a suspended sign displaying "MARKET RD." and one of four, abbreviated, cardinal compass points afterwards. Same asphalt. Roads widen into three-lanes on each side with turning lanes. Speed traps never drop below 45mph. Intersections show highway concurrencies four-bulb and FMs three-color protectors.

Cutoffs: Partial-access

Gated villages' main roads! Lay Otta seal. Give them two lanes on each side with a tree planter median. Intersections between switches double as U-turns too. Example: KEENAN CO. Limit top speed to 35mph. Place red, octagonal, stop signs at their exits.

Switches: Partial-access

Accesses rear parking and hamlet neighborhood blocks. Run Otta. Two-way roads have one lane on each side and create a teardrop-shaped loop around a grassy tree planter at their ends. Example: BROWN RD. (downtown); KAREN RD. A solid 25mph speed should do the trick! Stake a caution sign at the exits of their turnarounds to greet drivers merging back onto straightaways. Upon returning to the intersections of cutoffs, display yield signs on inverted triangles riveted to galvanized steel poles.

State Roads

Bypasses: Open-access

FM stands for farm-to-market. Farm roads link farms, shires and parishes together. All states should adopt Texas' FM system. Chip seal asphalt. Two-way roads post 75 mph speeds along state parks and 65 mph signage at shires. Within towns, junctions form concurrencies in residential areas and branches do the same at squares. Black signs display their state's shape in reverse font. Place compass signs above them.

Highway Interfaces

County Loops

Beltways: Controlled-access

Inner loops encircle limits with outskirts facing outward. Rubber asphalt composite. Five lanes each side cat 65 mph. Blue and gold pentagon signage. Example: BELT 610.

Greenways: Limited-access

Central loops envelop outer farmland. Chip seal. Four lanes on each side plus an open turning lane help push 70 mph. Post green and gold pentagons. Example: GREEN 8.

Parkways: Limited-access

Outer loops orbit state parkland. Chip seal. Three lanes each way also have a turning lane and can allocate 75 mph. Purple and gold pentagon signs. Example: PKWY 99. Originally, parkways were partial-access, scenic routes coursing through state and local park systems. Heavier trucks were restricted and forced onto alternate routes.

Highways

Interstate Freeways: Controlled-access

Rubber asphalt composite. Limit rural areas two-lanes each way without feeders capped at 85 mph. Anything beyond parkways are freeways get three lanes reduced to 75 mph. Two-lane feeders do straight-left and straight-right with 55 mph signage. Travelling past greenways result in four lanes donning 70 mph. Three-lane frontages showcase straight-left, straight and straight-right access permitting 50 mph. Passing beltways results in displays of five lanes given 65 mph. Feeders widen to accept left, straight-left, straight and straight-right running 45 mph. Don't forget about U-turns!

U.S. Motorways: Limited-access

Rubber asphalt. Rural areas are open-access. Urban sections demand composite beds and are controlled-access. Follow interstates' rules on lanes, feeders and speeds. However, never exceed 75 mph. Stake old-school signs from 1948. Example: US 59.

State Expressways: Limited-access

Rubber asphalt. Rural areas always get one-lane on both sides applying open access. Town concurrencies give way to two-lanes each side along branches and three at junctions. Urban sections passing parkways warrant three lanes (70 mph), two past greenways (65 mph) and four beyond beltways (60 mph). Prime example: SH 105.

Transits

Subways: Rapid Transit

Few people realize not everything is completely underground. Some sections do expose themselves to the public along aboveground bridgeways. Only megapolitan regions can afford to sustain them both financially and through overall population. All three mass transits listed connect their minor anchors together regardless of size.

Expresses: Light Rail

Unfortunately, we cannot afford a nationwide grid connecting every small town to its hub. Realistic expectations can be met with monorails in metros. Commuter rail only operates during rush hour in urban areas of hubs. Regional trains slow down to make numerous stops in the suburbs. Inter-city transits are express lines traveling at high speeds accessing the ring of minor anchor cities orbiting these metropolitans! High-speed rail (HSR) is divided into three main categories: Category I (155 mph+), Category II (124 mph+) and Category III where some railways dipping below 124 mph.

Trolleybuses: Tramway

Articulated buses remind me of accordions in the middle and replace rail lines with tires. They don't have to have overhead cable lines either. Although most are electric, future models could adopt turbocharged, biodiesel-electric engines with variable displacement. The British opted for double-decker buses instead. They're two-story vehicles. Private companies offer urban taxi and rural bus routes everywhere else.

Funiculars: Cableway

Pacific West Coast cities are famous for their efforts to keep old-school, cable-driven streetcars alive. Technology can give internal combustion engines an edge over them with variable drive, hybrid-electric motors, chargers and biofuel additives for public options. Yet, privatization of existing trams and cable grids can preserve history so our future generations can experience them too! Just sell tickets as compensation.

Airways

Airports: Municipal

Intercontinental airports (megas) fly international flights. National airlines (metros) cut across state lines. Regionals aren't present in every micropolis, just the ones forming micropolitan greaters. Urban counties also have recreational airfields too. Major hubs, including minor anchors, must be limited to one airfield per municipality.

Airfields: Countywide

Rural counties lack true airports, but still offer airfields to those commuting to their primary seats. Propellor planes and helicopters can be rented by the hour. Flight instructors serve as co-pilots and train students by teaching ground school classes.

Interior Routes

Park Systems

Unlike government roadways funded through taxes, privatized routes are tollways. Visitors must stop at a gated toll booth and buy a ticket to enter. Afterwards, they can access any road they want! Accept every form of payment from cash, coins, debit cards and credit cards. EZ tag memberships will benefit contractors, employees and rangers. Certain activities charge by the day. Hunting season has numerous rules too.

Byways: Open-access

Park highways, not to be confused with my county-run parkway loops. Chip seal. One lane each direction limited to 75 mph. Major hubs experience reductions down to 65 mph and hang yellow cautions. Park entrances have stone signs with red stoppers. Byways are marked by tan and white, flowerpot-shaped signage. Example: BWY 66.

Accesses: Open-access

Service routes for loggers, miners, etc. Wooden planks. Each side needs to be wide enough so semis can fit through them. Speed limits fluctuate from 55 mph all the way down to 45 mph. Monochromatic, rounded rectangular signs. Example: ROUTE 101.

Passes: Open-access

Refuges contain the campsites. Rock beds. One lane runs on both sides. Speed varies between 45 mph along straightaways to 35 mph along switch-shaped turnarounds. Example: EAGLE PASS. Post red and white yields riveted onto steel poles at all exits.

Trails: Open-access

Nature trails! Pea gravel helps control erosion and keeps footwear clean. Example: OREGON TRAIL. Yellow, diamond-shaped caution signs warn pedestrians of potential danger. Hikers, bikers and hunters should carry bear mace for protection. Mountain lion (.357 mag), black bear (.44 mag), brown bear (.454) and polar bear (.460) loads.

Route 66

Historic Byway: Open-access

America's main highway! Numerous state park systems are connected by this future tollway. Zoning laws allow businesses to buy frontage and market goods or services. Rubber asphalt. One lane on both sides unless encountering a concurrency. Paint iconic badges on them too. Speed limit is 75 mph bordering park systems, 65 mph through rural farmland and considerably less upon encountering concurrencies.

Review

Passages

Night Owls:

Construction crews operate under mobile, generator-powered lights during late-night graveyard shifts to reduce traffic. Not all truckers can do the same, especially those supplying culinary establishments. Gas stations with 24/7 service benefit from nocturnal deliveries. Some cities have highways prohibiting thru traffic. During the day, semis take alternate routes or could be forced onto feeders. Many only let them go 55 mph. In the future, truck stops replace more government-owned rest stops.

Defensive Driving:

Turning lanes require vehicles to come to a complete stop and wait for an opening before going. They're not hammer lanes nor are they accelerator ramps! Sometimes shoulders aren't present, lack substantial width or have obstacles present. That's the only time it's acceptable to stop in the slow lane before exiting. Otherwise, activate your blinker, slowly merge into it more and then round the corner without stopping.

Road Rage:

Convert hammer lanes dedicated to passing into fast lanes. HOV lanes suck. To me, they're HIV lanes. Higher speed limits reduce traffic better than widening roads with slower MPH signs. Municipal bonds should be enough to cover construction costs while taxes go towards maintenance. People already pay taxes, even those on welfare pay sales tax. So, don't impose tolls on government-owned infrastructure!

Patrols

Law Enforcement:

Towns get one sheriff, a mortician, two bailiffs and up to four deputies with five-pointed star badges. County judiciaries don police-style shield badges. They have one court constable, a coroner, two bailiffs and four deputies. City police forces need a pathologist. State rangers (judiciary type) and federal marshals are led by avenors.

CHAPTER SIX

Department of Air Force

<u>Quadrant 2:1</u>

Listed below is this chapter's section directory. Topics are grouped together in subsections labeled by underlined bullets. Any further subdivision of information is organized into verses marked by bolded bullets.

Overview

Alloys

Blueprints:

I invented six new metal alloys. You can use them for free! Aircraft frames are pure Alumax. This hot-forged aluminum superalloy contains aluminum, carbon, beryllium, scandium and praseodymium. Swap aluminum for magnesium in Alkalite and titanium in Tetmire. One is for NASA and trucking, the other medical equipment. Coat engine components in Tungmore. It's cast with tungsten, carbon, molybdenum and rhenium. Canopies are boron acrylic. Decks are coated with non-slip veneers of carbon fiber.

Landing Gear:

Undercarriages utilize Galmax, a hot-forged galvanized steel alloy with iron, carbon, manganese, vanadium and zinc. The zinc is not just a layer on top of the metal, it's also mixed inside of it too guaranteeing it will never rust. Coat anything visible with a thin veneer of Super Stainless, another hot-forged steel alloy. It contains the same elements as Galmax, but replaced its zinc with chromium (10-26% of the mixture).

Electronics:

Technology critical metals, some falling under the category of rare-earth elements, reduce how much precious metal is needed in electronics. Use tin/zinc solder, white brass insignia, yellow brass bullets and red brass plumbing fittings as alternatives to wasting raw copper. Conserving supplies makes them more affordable to civilians.

Airframes

Balanced Designs:

Heavy noses and light rear ends create balance. For wing designs, straight benefit drones, helicopters and biplanes. Ellipticals excelled on interwar period fighters. Compound shapes enhanced Vietnam-era and WWII fighters. Swept angles improved cargo planes' and Korean War fighter jets' performance. Swing-wings gave birth to supersonic bomber designs. Delta wings are for modern fighter and trainer jets.

Military Aircraft

Roster

*45,000 standing, 45,000 active guard, two air divisions and one space legion.

*U.S. Space Force becomes a legion operating the USAF's nuclear defense grid.

*Pratt & Whitney builds jet engines. General Dynamics supplies Vulcan ATCs.

*Cockpit styles: F-35 trainers, F-22 fighters, RAH-66 choppers, B-2 transports.

*Texas Instruments manufactures all avionics. Mount SNIPER and Legion pods.

*Autocannons fire 20mm Lake City ammunition. Buy Dillon Aero miniguns.

*Use Raytheon missiles and Holston Army Ammunition Plant explosives.

Inventory

200 Boeing F-15E Eagle x $48 million = $9.6 billion

USAF multirole strike fighters have two large, afterburning, turbofan engines and 20mm Vulcan ATCs. They run DAS (deep air support) striking factories and air bases. Install forward F-22 and rear F-35 seats. Strike Eagles also double as advanced trainers.

400 Lockheed Martin F-16C Viper x $30 million = $12 billion

USAF multirole, air superiority fighters get one large, afterburning, turbofan engine. Mount 13 weapons hardpoints and 20mm Vulcans. They escort strike fighters behind enemy lines and assist them in executing SEAD (suppression of enemy air defenses).

610 Lockheed Martin F-20 Tigershark x $18 million = $10.98 billion

Split between the navy and air force. Multirole interceptors rely on one medium-sized, afterburning, turbofan engine. In-flight refueling, nine external hardpoints, folding wings and carrier landing gear. Beefed up to house more electronics and greater fuel capacity. F-20s can perform SEAD, combat air patrols (CAP) and anti-piracy operations.

560 Northrop Grumman T-2 Buckeye x $4 million = $2.24 billion

T-2s are given carrier capable landing gear. Standardize one small, turbofan engine plus folding wings and unguided pylons. Install a forward F-22 and rear F-35 seat. Most focus on primary training, but naval versions also tackle advanced courses.

900 General Atomics MQ-1 Predator x $4 million = $3.6 billion

Divide 150 surveillance drones amongst all service branches. The remaining 750 serve as the Army's attack aircraft providing CAS (close air support) to regular ground units.

500 Bell AH-1W Super Cobra x $10.7 million = $5.99 billion

Shared by all service branches. Gives commandos CAS and covers UH-1N extractions. ATCs are triple-barreled 20mms. Equip Hellfire missiles on inner pylons, Hydra rockets along outer mounts and stingers at its wingtips. Needs two small, turboshaft engines.

800 Bell UH-1N Twin Huey x $4.7 million = $3.76 billion

Divided evenly between all branches. Performs SAR (search and rescue) and ASW (anti-submarine) patrols. Huey gunships cover commando extractions with their Dillon Aero miniguns. Gets two medium-sized, turboshafts and upgraded fuel tanks.

200 Sikorsky CH-54 Tarhe x $22 million = $4.4 billion

USN and U.S. Army cargo choppers. Resupplies and evacuates embassies from LHDs. Upgrades let units rival CH-53K King Stallions in performance letting them deploy greater payloads of towed field artillery or detachable universal pods than before. Needs two large turboshafts and more fuel capacity. Civilian versions are designated as S-64 Skycranes. Current models produced by Erickson, Inc. are known as Aircranes.

100 Boeing KC-135 Stratotanker x $4 million = $800 million

USAF's aerial refueling! Upgraded tanker jets are beefed up with four, medium-sized turbofans to upstage the overpriced KC-10 Extenders and KC-46 Pegasus prototypes.

250 Lockheed Martin C-130H Hercules x $7 million = $1.75 billion

Air supplies goods to USAF and U.S. Army. Unleashes bunker busters over hardened targets. While cargo helicopters airdrop artillery and infield relief along mountains, our cargo planes do the same to besieged frontline forces. AC-130 gunships and C-130J Super Hercules models cost too much to procure; avoid more and sell them off!

250 Sikorsky C-141C Starlifter x $18 million = $4.5 billion

USAF cargo plane. Inserts airborne paratroops (PJs) and delivers goods to overseas bases. Upgraded cockpits resemble C-5Ms. Propelled by four small, turbofan engines.

250 Lockheed Martin C-5M Galaxy x $100 million = $5 billion

USAF oversized cargo plane. Conquers outsized logistics, moves bases or delivers universal tanks to the battlefield. Reserved for the payloads the C-141s can't handle.

Total Aircraft = 5,070

Total Assets = $52.6 billion

USAF Rankings

Enlisted

Cadet: no rockers, blue-white star inside roundel – ground school/wingman E2

Private: single, blue-white rocker underneath a star roundel – trooper/beat E3

Corporal: two, blue-white rockers underneath star roundel – technician/detail E4

Sergeant: three, blue-white rockers underneath star roundel – element/section E5

Ensign: sergeant insignia, horizontal bar, specialty emblem – flight/troop E6

Commissioned

Commander: one, white brass leaf – air echelon/century (demi-company) OF4

Colonel: one, white brass eagle – air squadron/cohort (demi-battalion) OF5

Brigadier: one, white brass star – aviation wing/regiment (demi-brigade) OF6

Divisionnaire: one, white brass diamond – air group/legion (demi-division) OF7

General: one, white brass baton/wreath – air/infantry division (demi-corps) OF8

Administrative

Aide: elected politician, top retired general, tactical air force's NATO OF9

Adjutant: elected politician, top retired general, district air force's NATO OF10

Secretary: elected politician, top retired general, regular air force's NATO SPC

Elucidation

Generals advise HEADCOM, divisionnaires lead agencies and brigadiers run HQs. Garrison regiments at most air bases with cohorts manning outpost detachments. Administrators carry batons and secretaries receive machete swords. Only appoint aides and adjutants during major wars. Limit five adjutants per air force secretary.

Roman legions shrank in size as Roman civilization declined. On average, legions had 5,000 men arranged in 10 cohorts, the latter formation containing 60 centuries.

Centuries replaced maniples on the battlefield. Half-centuries numbered 50 men. Contuberniums were eight-man formations inspiring the squads we see today.

Regimental System

Aerial

Element: 1-2 aircraft, ensign

Flight: 2-4 aircraft, lieutenant

Echelon: 4-8 aircraft, commander

Squadron: 8-24 aircraft, colonel

Wing: 24-48 aircraft, brigadier

Aviation Group: -48-240 aircraft

Air Division: 240-1,000 aircraft

Tactical Force: 1,000-5,000 aircraft

District Force: 5,000-20,000 aircraft

Regular Force: 20,000-80,000+ aircraft

Aviation

Beat: 1-2 airman

Detail: 2-4 airmen

Crew: 4-10 airmen

Section: 10-20 airmen

Troop: 20-50 airmen

Century: 50-100 airmen

Cohort: 100-600 airmen

Regiment: 600-3,000 airmen

Legion: 3,000-10,000 airmen

Division: 10,000-40,000 airmen

Tactical: 40,000-150,000 airmen

District: 150,000-500,000 airmen

Organization

Subunit: Beat > Detail > Crew > Section *(Fire/Movement)*

Unit: Troop > Century > Cohort *(Skirmish Engagements)*

Formation: Regiment > Legion > Division *(Battlefields)*

Command: Tactical > District > Standing *(War Level)*

TACCOM: Tactical Force *(Wartime Operations)*

MAJCOM: District Force *(Wartime Strategies)*

HEADCOM: Regular Air Force *(USAF)*

Exposition

*Feudal lords held retinues of military servants to protect their fiefdoms. Colonels commanded smaller regiments and brigadiers bigger ones. Don't mix regimental and brigade systems together; it causes branches to need twice as many ranks!

Aircraft History

Mergers

Interceptor Fighter: *(Multirole fighter with shorter range and lighter payload)*

Light Fighter > Scout Fighter > Day Fighter > Fighter-bomber

Light Bomber > Torpedo Bomber > Dive Bomber > Attack Bomber

Air Superiority Fighter: *(Multirole fighter with moderate range and payload)*

Bomber Destroyer > Night Fighter > Intruder Fighter > Tactical Fighter

Medium Bomber > Night Bomber > Interdictor Bomber > Tactical Bomber

Strike Fighter: *(Multirole fighter with the longest range and heaviest payload)*

Heavy Fighter > Escort Fighter > Penetration Fighter (Cold War period)

Heavy Bomber > Strategic Bomber > Penetrator Bomber (supersonic/stealth)

Designs

Wing Shapes:

Straight (WWI) > Elliptical (interwar period) > Compound (WWII)

Swept (Korean War) > Swing-wing (Vietnam War) > Delta (Gulf War)

Air Superiority Fighter:

Radial > Inline > Ramjet > Turbojet/Turboprop > Turbofan/Turboshaft

Turboprop: Powers small cargo planes. Turbojets drive horizontal propellors.

Turboshaft: Goes on helicopters. They feature vertical props atop turbojets.

Turbocharger: Perfect on Predators' four-cylinder, inline, piston engines.

Battery: Loitering munitions rely on simple, battery-driven propellors.

Bomb Payloads:

Light Bomber: 500-1k lbs. WWI, 1k-2k lbs. interwar period, 2k-4k lbs. WWII

Medium Bomber: 1k-2klbs WWI, 2k-4k lbs. interwar period, 4k-8k lbs. WWII

Heavy Bomber: 2k-4klbs WWI, 4k-8k lbs. interwar period, 8k-22k lbs. WWII

Strategic Bomber: 22k-44k lbs. WWII, 44k-70k lbs. Korean/Cold War period

Penetrator Bomber: 21k-75k lbs. Vietnam War, 75k-125k lbs. Gulf War

Review

Future Wars

Rank Realignment:

Newbies must enlist regardless of education level. Doing so renders rocker sergeants who babysat inexperienced officers unnecessary. Enlistees select a specialty putting an end to specialist forever. Not all countries' militaries considered their cornets and ensigns officer ranks. Academies give subalterns (O1) one bar, lead lieutenants (O2) two and majors (O3) three. Becoming skilled in a professional trade eliminates warrant officers. Three elected officials replace general officers beyond NATO OF8.

Wartime Budgets:

Spend no more than $500 billion USD on aircraft assets for your entire military during any future world war. With proper inflation adjustments, this was how much our WWII aircraft inventory was worth in FY2024. In addition to paying down our existing national debt figures, we need to issue Series EE war bonds once war breaks loose.

Birds of Prey

Penetrator Bombers:

Cargo planes carry bunker busters and nuclear cruise missiles. Smaller, affordable, HMX-filled, guided ordinance loaded aboard fighter jets is the way. Place unnecessary aircraft in military museums to conduct air shows. During wars, the USAF leases them!

Obsolete Aircraft:

Hunter subs replaced the anti-submarine patrol role of P-8s. SR-71s rendered RC-135s obsolete before satellites replaced them too. Drones did the same to early warning aircraft. Giving each fighter jet an ECM pod eliminates the need for Growlers.

Presidential Travel:

Make Air Force One a Gulfstream G800 jet. Marine One is just one Sikorsky VH-60N White Hawk helicopter. We don't need an echelon of aircraft to ensure his safety!

CHAPTER SEVEN

Department of Navy

Quadrant 2:2

Listed below is this chapter's section directory. Topics are grouped together in subsections labeled by underlined bullets. Any further subdivision of information is organized into verses marked by bolded bullets.

Overview

Shipyards

Refurbishment:

It's cheaper to build new ships using older classes, upgrade them and decorate them to look like the new designs we like. Buying out excess naval warship museums and remodeling them saves money, which explains why my costs are so low. The U.S. Navy leases our battleship museums during major wars. Cannibalization saves money too.

Fusion Reactors:

Deuterium is converted to tritium in lithium-lined vacuum chambers called tokamaks. Magnets control plasma hotter than our Sun! Uses helium (primary) and molten salt (secondary) cooling. Tungsten carbide and steel shielding prevents combat damage.

Auxiliary Militia:

Saltwater refineries provide the USN and U.S. Merchant Marine all their hydrogen, oxygen, salt, helium and D-T isotopes. Hydrogen and oxygen power their boilers' pilot lights. Freshwater fills the tanks and provides crews with potable water. These boilers generate steam for their turbines. Naval landing craft are powered by turbocharged, hydrogen engines accompanied by variable displacement and hybrid-electric motors.

Metallurgy

Solid Construction:

Construct hulls out of hot-forged Galmax. Anything visible to the outside world is coated in Super Stainless. Decks are topped by a thin veneer of non-slip carbon fiber. Critical components on all surface vessels are protected by a series of Kevlar panels.

Key Components:

Use tin/zinc solder, white brass insignia, yellow brass bullets and red brass plumbing fittings as alternatives to wasting raw copper. Run waste water through PVC. Exterior windows have boron additives. Their HMX-filled ordinance is half the size and cost!

Watercraft Totals

80,000 active, 80,000 reserve, two USN squadrons and two USMC divisions. Bath Ironworks builds ships, Hunting Ingalls subs, Huckins boats and ELCO smaller craft, Install General Atomics D-T fusion reactors and Texas Instruments electronics. The entire U.S. Merchant Marine is already their auxiliary fleet; ditch the NFAF!

Warships

4 Enterprise CVN x $2.4 billion = $9.6 billion

110k tons x 4 = 440k tons

Given wider frames, two thorium reactors and Ford-class upgrades. Armored flight decks capitalize on ceramic plates saving weight. CISWs and SAMs come standard. F-20 Tigersharks fly CAP, SEAD and anti-piracy operations around all naval squadrons.

6 Essex LHD x $1.2 billion = $7.2 billion

45k tons x 6 = 270k tons

Remodel the Essex museums into LHDs with STOBAR (ski-jump runways) and fusion reactors. Use CIWS (close-in weapons systems) and SAM (surface-to-air missiles) missiles. LHDs (landing helicopter docks) land LCM landing craft filled with marines. Hueys serve as their medivacs while Tarhe choppers resupply coastal U.S. embassies.

8 Kidd CG x $260 million = $2.08 billion

10k tons x 8 = 80k tons

Redesign Spruance-class destroyers to look like Ticonderogas. Aegis ballistic defense computers coordinate boomers' missiles. Install composite armor and 8" turrets for shore bombardment. Load SAMs, CISWs, Harpoon ship missiles and Mk-54 torpedoes.

52 Hazard DDG x $130 million = $6.76 billion

4k tons x 48 = 192k tons

Remodel short-hulled frigates to resemble Arleigh Burke destroyers with reactors. They fire 6" cannonry at enemy patrols and deploy Proteus MCMV submersibles. Equip harpoon ASMs, SAMs, CISWs, Mk-54 torpedoes and lighter plating than a Kidd.

48 Claud Jones DEG x $65 million = $3.12 billion

2k tons x 48 = 96k tons

Destroyer escort frigates look like the Constellation class and have reactors too! Units fire 4"cannons at pirates to defend civilian ships. Loadouts incorporate Harpoons, SAMs, CISWs, Mk-54 torpedoes and thinner armor plating than Hazard destroyers.

18 Higgins LCU x $25 million = $450 million

1k tons x 18 = 18k tons

Higgins boats! Landing craft utilities deploy marine IFVs onto beaches and cover them with smaller, C4-filled Hydra rockets. Twin-supers, fuel rails and blower on 36L V16.

72 Mike LCM x $3 million = $216 million

120 tons x 72 = 8,640 tons

Mike boats! Landing craft mechanized unload marine vehicles further upriver.They protect everyone with .50cal, M2A1 machine guns. Similar engine, but it's an 18L V12.

96 Zodiac STAB x $100 thousand = $9.6 million

4 tons x 96 = 384 tons

Rubber "strike" assault boats carry USMC Raiders upriver and support them with their general purpose, 7.62mm, M204B machine guns. Similar engine, but it's a 7.2L V10.

12 Columbia II SSBN x $130 million = $1.56 billion

4k tons x 12 = 48k tons

Sub museums receive Columbia-class upgrades and Trident III ballistic missiles for ASAT (Anti-satellite) and ABM (anti-ballistic) duties, along with new Mk-48 torpedoes.

56 Seawolf II SSN x $65 million = $3.64 billion

2k tons x 56 = 112k tons

Sub museums are given Seawolf-class upgrades, Harpoons, Mk-48s and SEAL SDVs. Targets for surface fleet, escorts boomers and deploys SEAL Team's submersibles.

52 Proteus MCMV x $40 thousand = $2.08 million

1 ton x 52 = 48 tons

Mine countermeasure ROVs help our destroyers spot enemy attack submarines and clear minefields. They combine traditional mine hunting and minesweeping together.

6 Mark VIII SSN x $800 thousand = $4.8 million

17 tons x 6 = 102 tons

SEAL Teams' deployment vehicles are submersibles manned by scouting frogmen.

Total Watercraft = 430 Units

Total Tonnage = 1,265,174

Total Assets = $34.6 billion

USN Rankings

Enlisted

Apprentice: two white anchors underneath eagle – ground school/mate E2

Seaman: inverted silver chevron above two white anchors and eagle – beat E3

Yeoman: two, inverted silver chevrons above anchors and eagle – detail E4

Boatswain: three, inverted silver chevrons above anchors and eagle – crew E6

Midshipman: silver rocker placed on top of boatswain insignia – section E6

Commissioned

Commander: one, white brass leaf – station/century (task element) OF4

Captain: one, white brass eagle – sector/cohort (task echelon) OF5

Commodore: one, white brass star – flotilla/regiment, (task unit) OF6

Divisionnaire: one, white brass diamond – naval division (task group) OF7

Admiral: one, white brass baton/wreath – naval squadron (task force) OF8

Administrative

Aide: elected politician, top retired admiral, standing fleet's NATO OF9

Adjutant: elected politician, top retired admiral, combined fleet's NATO OF10

Secretary: elected politician, top retired admiral, regular navy's NATO SPC

Elucidation

*Admirals advise HEADCOM, divisionnaires lead agencies and commodores run HQs. Garrison sectors at bases with stations anchored along outpost detachments. Administrators receive batons and secretaries ceremonial machete swords. Only elect aides and adjutants during major conflicts. Limit five adjutants per secretary.

*Squadrons are defined by how many aircraft, vehicles, artillery pieces, boats or ships they operate. Most branches staff a cohort's worth of men under a colonel. There are less ships than other types of vehicles, but they require more personnel. Naval squadrons have tens of thousands of sailors led by a three-star admiral!

Naval History

Ships of Line

Trimester Periods:

Pre-ironclad (man-of-war) > Semi-ironclad (teak) > Post-ironclad (Siemens)

Development Transitions:

Man-of-War > Broadside Battery > Barbette Battery (*floating batteries*)

Frigate > Broadside Frigate > Barbette Frigate (*ironclad battleships*)

Corvette > Broadside Corvette > Barbette Corvette (*station ironclads*)

Sloop-of-war > Broadside Sloop > Barbette Sloop (*ocean-going monitors*)

Bomb Ketch > Casemate Gunboat > Breastwork Monitor (*coastal monitors*)

Fireboat (hellfire boat) > Casemate Ram > Light Draft Monitor (*gunboats*)

Unrated Warships:

Stores Ship > Barracks Hulk > Collier > Balloon Tender > Mine Planter

Bomb Ketch: Mortar vessels bombarded coastal forts with heavy mortars.

Aviso: Prior to the telegraph, dispatch boats delivered messages to ships.

Battleships

Trimester Periods:

Pre-dreadnought > Semi-dreadnought > Post-dreadnought (all-big-gun)

Development Transitions:

Pre-dreadnought > Semi-dreadnought > Dreadnought (1st class battleships)

Armored Cruiser > Light Cruiser > Heavy Cruiser (1st class cruisers)

Protected Cruiser > Scout Cruiser > Destroyer Leader (2nd class cruisers)

Unprotected Cruiser (3rd Class) > Torpedo Gunboat > Torpedo Boat Destroyer

Torpedo Ram > Torpedo Cruiser (unrated cruisers) > Torpedo Boat

Coastal Submarine > Midget Submarine > Human Torpedo (submersible)

Unrated Warships:

Barracks, Depot Ship, Oiler, Auxiliary Cruiser, Minelayer, Minesweeper

Future Fleets

Carrier Era

Trimestral Periods:

Pre-WWII (interwar period) > World War II > Post-WWII (Post-Cold War)

Development Transitions:

Aircraft Carrier: Light Carrier (small) > Escort Carrier (slow) > Fleet Carrier

Amphibious Warfare Ship: Attack Cargo Ship > Landing Ship > Assault Ship

1. Amphibious Cargo Ship: *LSI (infantry) > LSM (medium) > LSV (vehicle)*

2.Landing Ship: *LST (tank) > LSD (dock) > LPD (platform, aka transport)*

3. Amphibious Assault Ship: *LPH (platform) > LHA (assault) > LHD (dock)*

Landing Craft (infantry): LCP (personnel R/L) > LCI (infantry L/S) > LCU (utility)

Landing Craft (vehicles): LCV (vehicle/person) > LCT (tank) > LCM (mechanized)

Landing Vehicle: LVT (vehicle tracked) > LCA (assault) > IFV (infantry fighting)

Assault Craft: Storm Boat (wooden) > Raiding Craft (rubber) > Strike Boat "STAB"

Mine Warfare: Minesweeper > Minehunter > Mine Countermeasures Vessel

Battleship: Super-Dreadnought > Fast Battleship > Joint Support Ship (JSS)

Cruiser: Aircraft Cruiser > Large/Command Cruiser > Guided-missile Cruiser

Destroyer: Fleet Destroyer > Destroyer Escort > Guided-missile Destroyer

Attack Sub: Cruiser Sub (big) > Fleet Sub (med) > Hunter-Killer Sub (small)

Boomer Sub: Aircraft Sub > Tanker Sub > Arsenal Sub (cruise/ballistic missile)

Diver Propulsion Vehicle: Dry Sub (cabin) > Wet Sub (exposed) > SDV (wet)

Battleships

Standard Ratings:

What we call battleships are 1st class battleships, or coastal assault battleships. Modern cruisers originated as 2nd class battleships, aka cruising battleships or cruiser battleships. Battlecruiser was a nickname given to larger armored cruisers. Large cruisers originated as a way to let America's Alaska-class cheat WWII naval treaties. Russia's Kirov-class aren't battlecruisers because they lack large cannon batteries.

Review

Future Wars

Wartime Budgets:

Spend no more than $250 billion USD on naval assets during any future world war. Never exceed 8,000 watercraft totaling 8 million tons in max deep load displacement. With inflation adjustment, the WWII U.S. Navy was worth that in FY2024 figures. Merchant marines can covert their ships into auxiliary cruisers whenever necessary.

Museum Conversions:

Naval museum projects are led by Seabees, USCG cutter exhibits the Civil Engineering Program and USAF airshows RED HORSE squadron. What they lack in manpower is compensated by the Army Corps of Engineers. Leave a handful of each for tourists and buy out the rest. Install D-T reactors, remodel towers, replace turrets and upgrade electronics. Replace armor with lighter composites and sell off excess steel.

Stealthier Submarines:

The last true hunter-killer (2,000-4,000 tons) the U.S. built was the Barracuda class. This was developed shortly after WWII, a time when we had Tench class submarines. Listed below are the ideal tonnage ranges displayed in max deep load displacement.

Naval Escorts

Large Cruiser: 10,000 to 28,000 tons

Guided Cruiser: 4,000 to 10,000 tons

Guided Destroyer: 2,000 to 4,000 tons

Guided Frigate: 1,000 to 2,000 tons

Guided Corvette: 500 to 1,000 tons

Mine Warfare: under 1,000 tons

Fast Attack Craft: under 500 tons

Cruiser Sub: 4,000 to 10,000 tons

Boomer Sub: 2,000 to 4,000 tons

Hunter-Killer: 1,000 to 2,000 tons

Coastal Sub: 500 to 1,000 tons

Minelayer Sub: 200 to 500 tons

Midget Sub: under 150 tons

ROV Drone: under 10 tons

CHAPTER EIGHT

Department of Army

Quadrant 2:3

Listed below is this chapter's section directory. Topics are grouped together in subsections labeled by underlined bullets. Any further subdivision of information is organized into verses marked by bolded bullets.

Overview

Vehicles

Affordable Alloys:

Galmax is affordable, cheaper to repair and recyclable compared to fiberglass. Semi cabs employ Alkalite tops to prevent rollovers. V-shaped hulls on vehicles ensure superior IED protection. Replace expensive titanium parts in M777s with my Alumax.

Reactive Matrixes:

We no longer need to slap depleted uranium on top of hardened steel! Pour the rest of our stocks as DUCRETE (DU concrete) and sell it to businesses. Main battle tanks should only weigh 50 tons. My composite armor consists of Tetmire backing plates, boron carbide tiles stuffed in matrixes and outer exploding panels to deflect impacts.

Critical Components:

Use tin/zinc solder, white brass insignia, yellow brass bullets and red brass plumbing fittings as alternatives to raw copper. Add boron to glass. To make artillery systems more affordable, ditch digital guidance systems, armor, treads and titanium alloys.

Efficient Engines:

Variable displacement shuts down cylinders while cruising and hybrid electric engines take over whenever vehicles are idling. This could quadruple fuel economy! Exhaust silencers added onto existing mufflers allow diesels to be as quiet as gas turbines. Injecting diesel exhaust fluid (DEF) reduces smog making tank crews harder to spot.

Munitions

Plastic Explosives:

Shells and C4 contain mixtures of RDX. Tank cannons are 120 mm wide. Anti-tank sabots are high velocity, fin-stabilized, depleted uranium darts coated in pyrophoric substances. MBTs fire HEAT rounds at everything else. Howitzers are fed 6.1" HE shells and the U.S. Navy loads AP ammunition; both options come standard with steel tips.

Military Vehicles

Standing

150,000 standing actives, 150,000 active guard, two generals and two corps.

Field armies and army groups are only used wartime. USMC adopts similar ranks.

Hybrid electric, variable-displacement engines with B7 biodiesel blends and DEF.

General Dynamics cannons and rocket launchers. Again, HSAAP supplies RDX.

Install Texas Instruments electronics and M2A2 QCBs on Browning M2A1s.

Watervliet Arsenal cannons and Milwaukee Tool with tungsten carbide bits.

Inventory

15,000 General Motors M48A6 Patton MBT x $300 thousand = $4.5 billion

U.S. Army's 50-ton, main battle tanks! Turrets house 120mm cannons, come stocked with SABOT and HEAT rounds, house coaxial 7.62mm M240Bs to repel infantry and are topped with belt-fed, .50cal M2A1 barbettes to destroy aerial threats. Ammo racks compartmentalize fires behind crews. Retreating tanks and cavalry units launch smoke grenades to cover their movements. Twin-turbo, 7.5L V8s crank out 1,000 hp.

200 FMC M113A4 Wolverine II AVLB x $300 thousand = $60 million

U.S. Army's 18-ton, armored bridge tanks! Armored, vehicle-launched bridge (ALVB) units fire det cord to eliminate minefields ahead of units. IED-resistant V-hulls and eight, run-flat tires reduce maintenance. Twin-turbo, 6.5L V8s will ensure 50-55 mph.

35,000 FMC M113A5 Bradley II IFV x $300 thousand = $10.5 billion

Shared by U.S. Army and Marine Corps. Infantry fighting vehicles resemble Strykers! Stock 20mm chain guns, coaxial M240Bs and M2A1 HMG barbettes. Give them eight, run-flat tires and IED-resistant V-hulls. Twin-turbo, 6.5L V8s guarantee 50-55 mph.

13,000 Fiat Chrysler Growler II ISV x $8 thousand = $1.04 billion

Split between U.S. Army and Marine Corps. Internal security vehicles are affordable alternatives to our aging fleet of overpriced Humvees! These 4x4 sand rails are lightly-armored cars carrying M240Bs during patrol duty. Its 80-mph performance is the byproduct of compact 2.5L, twin-turbo, inline, four-cylinder, small block engines.

10,000 Fiat Chrysler Humvee II IMV x $24 thousand = $240 million

Armored jeeps for everyone! Half of these Wrangler JLs tote mortars and the others, MK19 grenade launchers. A 3.5L, twin-turbo, V6 engine reaches speeds over 90 mph.

8,500 Rock Island Arsenal M777A1 Excalibur x $250 thousand = $2.13 billion

U.S. Army's towed field artillery. Medium howitzers are stationed at outposts and at bases along mountainous areas. They also load the same unguided 6", HE rounds as SPGs. During winter conditions, batteries initiate avalanches as a safety precaution.

3,500 Ford M270A2 Patriot II MLRS x $200 thousand = $700 million

U.S. Army MLRS. Multiple-launch, rocket systems are loaded aboard F550 Super Duty dually models with M270 turrets installed in their truck beds. Big blocks in the form of 6.5L, twin-turbo, V8 engines offer the perfect balance of horsepower and torque!

6,500 Ford M108A1 Paladin II SPG x $150 thousand = $975 million

U.S. Army self-propelled guns are stationed at camps as offensive "shoot-and-scoot" units. F650 Super Duties are dually pickups firing unguided, HE artillery shells through palatized 6" howitzers. Its twin-turbo, 7.5L V8 engine blocks are absolute necessities.

6,000 Ford F750 Deuce x $80 thousand = $480 million

Barracks trucks shared by all service branches. Five-ton dually trucks are given long axles with covered beds to move reinforcements into positions. Some vehicles are modified to fulfill the role of medivacs. Needs twin-turbocharged, 8.5L, V8 engines.

4,000 Mack Granite x $100 thousand = $400 million

Cargo trucks split between the four major branches. Ten-ton semis have a built-in PLS (palletized loading system) for dry cargo loads. Cargo containers divide into crates containing boxes further optimizing organization. Twin-turbo, 10.5L, inline six engines.

2,000 Mack Pinnacle x $120 thousand = $240 million

Wet cargo trucks for all branches! Twenty-ton cabs tow tanker trailers filled with fuel, oil or potable water. If French fries shouldn't be fried in oil used to cook fish, then the same principle applies to trailers. Demands twin-turbo, 12.5L, inline sixes as engines.

1,000 Mack Anthem x $150 thousand = $150 million

Split evenly between branches. Semis deploy wrecker systems and carry oversized cargo aboard trailers. This Anthem isn't their 20-ton version, it's a custom, 40-ton, military option! Mandatory use of twin-turbo, 14.5L, inline sixes to get work done!

Total Vehicles = 213,200

Total Assets = $21.4 billion

Army Rankings

Enlisted

Buck: star decal patch – boot camp/artillery matross (battle buddy) E2

Private: one black chevron – CQC rifleman/bayonet combat (tag team) E3

Corporal: two black chevrons – CQB infantryman/breaching (fireteam) E4

Sergeant: three black chevrons – gunner/grenadier specialist (squad) E5

Cornet: sergeant insignia, rocker, specialty emblem – sniper (platoon) E6

Commissioned

Commander: one, white brass leaf – company (outpost detachment) OF4

Colonel: one, white brass eagle – battalion (garrisoned base/column) OF5

Brigadier: one, white brass star – brigade (district headquarters base) OF6

Divisionnaire: one, white brass diamond – division (administration) OF7

General: one, white brass baton/wreath – corps (regional command) OF8

Administrative

Aide: elected politician, top retired general, field army's NATO OF9

Adjutant: elected politician, top retired general, army group's NATO OF10

Secretary: elected politician, top retired general, regular army's NATO SPC

Elucidation

Generals advise HEADCOM, divisionnaires lead agencies and brigadiers run HQs. Garrison battalions at most bases with companies manning outpost detachments. Administrators carry batons and secretaries receive machete swords. Only appoint aides and adjutants during major wars. Limit five adjutants per U.S. Army secretary.

Smaller militaries appointed lieutenant colonels as camp aides, but larger ones made the role a four-star endeavor. Adjutants were originally any officer second in command to a unit. Adjutant generals in the Russian Imperial Army sometimes held ranks of field marshal (five-star)! Secretaries are equal to special grades (SPCs).

Brigade System

Formations

Tag Team: 1-2 soldiers

Fireteam: 2-4 soldiers

Squad: 4-16 soldiers

Platoon: 16-100 soldiers

Company: 100-300 soldiers

Battalion: 300-1,500 soldiers

Brigade: 1,500-10,000 soldiers

Division: 10,000-40,000 soldiers

Corps: 40,000-150,000 soldiers

Field: 150,000-500,000 soldiers

Group: 500,000-2mil soldiers

Region: 2mil-8mil+ soldiers

Examples

Tag Team: DMR Team

Fireteam: CQB Team

Squad: Artillery Crew

Platoon: Contingent

Company: Detachment

Battalion: Commandos (SF)

Brigade: Fire Support (Artillery)

Division: Armor (MBT Vehicles)

Corps: Cavalry (IMV Vehicles)

Field: Nationalized Command

Group: Continental Command

Region: Coalition Command

Organization

Subunit: Tag Team, Fireteam, Squad *(Fire/Movement)*

Unit: Platoon, Company, Battalion *(Skirmish Level)*

Formation: Brigade, Division, Corps *(Battlefields)*

Command: Field, Group, Region *(War Level)*

TACCOM: Field Army *(Tactical Wartime)*

MAJCOM: Army Group *(Major Wartime)*

HEADCOM: Regular Army (U.S. Army)

Exposition

*Bucket brigades are chains of people passing items between one another. Chain gangs are lines of prisoners shackled together to perform hard labor for society.

Army History

Vehicles

Axle Ratings:

Two: Front-wheel Drive (4x2) > Rear-wheel Drive (4x2) > Four-wheel Drive (4x4)

Three: Two-wheel Drive (6x2), Four-wheel Drive (6x4), All-wheel Drive (6x6)

Four: Four-wheel Drive (8x4) > Six-wheel Drive (8x6) > All-wheel Drive (8x8)

Cavalry Units:

APC: Armored Transport (prisons/banks) > Half-track > IFV (infantry fighting)

Armored Car: Scout Car > Reconnaissance Vehicle > IMV (infantry mobility)

Tactical Vehicle: LUV (light utility) > LAV (light attack) > ISV (internal security)

Tank Classes:

Heavy Tank: Super-Heavy Tank > Assault Gun > Main Battle Tank (universal tank)

Medium Tank: Infantry Tank > Tank Destroyer > Main Battle Tank (universal tank)

Light Tank: Tankette > Cruiser Tank (fast) > Main Battle Tank (universal tank)

Hobart's Funnies: Flame Tank > DD Tank > Assault Breacher (bridge tank)

Artillery

Battery Sizes:

Army Cannon: Heavy (over 6.1") > Medium (4.1-6.1") > Light (20 mm to 4.1")

Naval Rifle: Large (above 8"), Heavy (7-8") > Light (5-6") > Small (under 5")

Grenade Launcher: Large (80mm) > Medium (40mm) > Small (20mm)

Artillery Evolution:

Mountain: Pack Gun (mule) > Recoilless Rifle (rockets) > Grenade Carrier (SPA)

Battlefield: Field Gun ("birch") > Anti-tank Gun (towed) > Mortar Carrier (SPA)

Siege Gun: Large SPG (above 8") > Heavy SPG (6.1-8") > Medium SPG (4.1-6.1")

Garrison Gun: Large TFA (above 8") > Heavy TFA (6.1-8") > Medium TFA (4.1-6")

Coastal Battery: Large Mortar (above 8") > Large Gun (above 8") > MLRS (SSM)

Review

Future Wars

Wartime Budgets:

During a world war, keep ground assets set to a maximum of 3 million vehicles with a value no greater than $120 billion USD. With proper inflation adjustment, our WWII army was worth that amount in FY2024 currency. You can maintain this budget and stockpile the same number of fighting vehicles, but don't build too many dually trucks or semis. Bulk up on the cheaper light trucks, jeep models or preferably, sand rails. MARS Radio coordinates additional logistical and engineering whenever necessary.

Armored Fists

Ground and Pound:

The real reason we need this much armor compared to before is because I'm using less CAS (close air support). Outside of special forces missions, it is too costly and time consuming. Commandos perform HALO drops, capitalize on drone assistance and extract via helicopter. Infantrymen place more emphasis on unguided artillery.

Firing for an Effect:

Guided STAFF rounds are 60x more expensive than dumb (unguided) HE shells! Compared to missiles, they don't generate a smoke cloud obscuring vision and giving away battery positions to enemy spotters. Howitzers reload faster than MLRS units and towed pieces fit in steep terrain where nothing else is possible. Ammo is much smaller allowing crews to carry more of it. Rocket artillery has more range, but isn't as cheap. MLRS is limited to counter-battery fire operations to outrange enemy arty.

Armored Fighting Vehicles:

MBTs were originally intended to weigh no more than medium tanks (50 tons). IFVs replaced light tanks when it comes to beach landings because most are capable of being amphibious. For defense positions, outposts station vehicles dubbed grenade carriers alongside SPGs. Bases garrison mortar carriers to defend MLRS batteries.

CHAPTER NINE

Department of CBP

Quadrant 2:4

Listed below is this chapter's section directory. Topics are grouped together in subsections labeled by underlined bullets. Any further subdivision of information is organized into verses marked by bolded bullets.

Overview

Vessels

Compact Designs:

Coast guards are supposed to be boat squadrons, not fleets of ships! They're way too big! With the advent of affordable fusion reactors, any vessel beyond 1,000 tons could have affordable nuclear power. High endurance corvettes are powered by hydrogen boilers and steam turbines. Coastal speedboats and inland watercraft benefit from superchargers. River ferries need turbochargers. Cutters are fiberglass while lifeboats have inflatable rubber hulls. This reduces their classes' displacement.

Hydrogen Power:

Saltwater refineries conduct electrolysis to supply our civilians hydrogen, oxygen and freshwater. Oxygen allows hydrogen to burn to power boilers' pilot lights. Freshwater fills these tanks, which generates steam for turbine shafts. Boats run on hydrogen to power inboard or outboard motors. USCG is a brown-water squadron, U.S. Merchant Marine America's green-water supply fleet and USN our country's blue-water fleet.

Defining Watercraft:

A vessel is an umbrella term ranging from arteries, urns, etc. Watercraft is defined as anything traveling through water. Craft include manned torpedoes. Boats never ship out to other continents. Therefore, that's why ferries, river cruises and coastal vessels shouldn't be placed in this niche category. Ships measure at least 100-200 ft, lean the opposite direction of their turns and can carry boats. Corvettes are oceangoing ships.

Boats

Engine Blocks:

Lifeboats rely on hydrogen-powered,twin-supercharged, hybrid electric engines with variable cylinder displacement. Ideal block sizes include 36L V16s offshore, 18L V12s nearshore and 7.2L V10s inshore. Make USCG cutters resemble Legends, Heritages, Sentinels and Protectors. Some will be corvettes, others designated patrol vessels.

CBP Realignment

<u>U.S. Coast Guard</u> (40,000 privateers)

4 Bolinger Erie x $34 million = $136 million

1,000 tons x 4 = 4,000 tons

National security corvettes are green-water ships escorting the NSF. Historically, Eries and Eagles were boats, not ships. They're the epitome of soft power letting them access treaty-restricted Antarctica. Each one has an air hanger, 57mm cannon, CISW, set of Mk-54 torpedo launchers and six Browning M2A1s stationed within barbettes.

80 Bolinger Eagle x $16 million = $1.28 billion

500 tons x 80 = 40,000 tons

Deepwater corvettes are green-water ships shadowing U.S. cruise lines. They have an aviation hanger, 35mm cannon, CISW, Mk-54 pod and four Browning M2A1s. Helicopter patrols allow these corvettes to stay out of visible range from their targets.

48 Elco Ashville x $8 million = $768 million

200 tons x 48 = 9,600 tons

PSMM Mk5s are offshore patrol vessels tasked with monitoring the conditions of oil rigs. Needs one HELO pad, 25mm gun, Mk-54 torpedo pod and two Browning M2A1s.

84 Elco Chaser x $4 million = $336 million

100 tons x 84 = 8,400 tons

PC-1610 inshore patrol vessels deter poaching fishermen with one M2A1 barbette.

160 Elco Dog x $2 million = $320 million

50 tons x 160 = 8,000 tons

Dog boats serve as fast patrol vessels monitoring reefs. Give them M240B MMGs!

32 Huckins Launch x $1 million = $32 million

25 tons x 32 = 800 tons

Convert WW2 Launch boats to all-weather lifeboats perfect for offshore rescues!

48 Huckins Swift x $500k = $24 million

10 tons x 48 = 480 tons

Swift boats become their all-weather lifeboats executing inshore rescues.

NOAA Survey

16 Bolinger Hamilton x $160 million = $2.56 billion

5,000 tons x 16 = 80,000 tons

Block II Hamilton ships monitor weather, clean up oil spills and remove litter. Deep-diving ROVs eradicate invasive sea life. They can also restore reefs and breed fish too! Let's salvage metal or increase predatorial species to protect aquatic environments!

NSF Research

1 Marinette Marine Mercy II x $300 million = $300 million

72,000 tons x 1 = 72,000 tons

Hospital ship provides humanitarian aid and medical care for the U.S. Navy. Mercy II is a helicopter carrier with STOVL catapults, but it's not an amphibious assault ship.

1 Marinette Marine Polaris x $400 million = $400 million

36,000 tons x 1 = 36,000 tons

Polar class 1 (PC-1) icebreaker. Resupplies Antarctic research stations regardless of weather conditions. Exchange seeds with park systems in the Southern hemisphere.

1 Marinette Marine Healy x $200 million = $200 million

18,000 tons x 1 = 16,000 tons

PC-2 icebreaker. Resupplies Arctic research bases and clears routes throughout the Great Lakes all-year round. Healy participates in the Holarctic realm's seed exchange.

Customs & Border Patrol (6,000 agents)

The immigration office handles work visas, border patrol patrols our boundaries, customs searches vehicles at checkpoints and ICE teams perform raids. USCG uses my naval ranks while other government agencies study my CBP "police" rank systems.

Total Peace Officers = 46,000 people

Total Watercraft = 523 vessels

Total Assets = $6.4 billion

CBP Rankings

Enlisted

Rookie: CBP emblem, service uniform – police academy/PTO (partner) E2

Private: one black chevron, service uniform – trooper/patrolman (beat) E3

Corporal: two black chevrons/uniform – HRT operator/breaching (detail) E4

Sergeant: three black chevrons/uniform – grenadier/demolitions (crew) E5

Cornet: sergeant insignia, rocker, specialty emblem – SWAT sniper (troop) E6

Commissioned

Detective: one, white brass leaf/business casual – station commander OF4

Inspector: one, white brass eagle/business casual – sector base/squadron OF5

Superintendent: one, white brass star/business informal – regional precinct OF6

Deputy: one, white brass diamond/business informal – division agency OF7

Chief: one, white brass baton/business informal – national bureau OF8

Elucidation

*Chiefs advise HEADCOM, deputies are agency administrators and superintendents run HQs. Garrison precinct bases and station outposts. The Dept. of CBP appoints commissioners instead of secretaries. They're issued batons, but won't receive machete swords. The CBP's irregular system is smaller than the regimental system.

*Any enlisted agent holding the rank of corporal or above is a non-commissioned officer (NCO). Detectives in most police departments can vary in rank from corporal all the way to captain, but only special agents in charge (SAIC) reach commander. Some countries use the titles chief inspector (OF6) and chief superintendent (OF7).

*USCG's squadron has one admiral, two divisions and four flotillas. The border patrol's bureau hires one chief overseeing the customs and border patrol agencies.

*USCG ranks match USN versions. For enlisted insignia, give fatigues silver, blue dress white and white dress black patches. This applies to the navy too. Marine personnel adopt red versions of my army's ranks. Army dress uniforms don yellow chevrons. U.S. Space Legion's monochromatic patches opt for inverted chevrons!

Review

Irregulars

Paramilitary Action:

U.S. Customs and Border Patrol is a federal law enforcement agency. Unlike a police force of marshals, they're the militarized version called privateers. Our CBP is still rated as a paramilitary force because they lack the firepower of a regular military armed forces branch, yet have more presence than most SWAT teams deployed by local police departments. Their irregular formation system is much smaller than the U.S. Air Force's regimental system and smaller than the U.S. Army's brigade system.

CBP Explorers:

Right now, this CBP auxiliary branch is considered nothing more than a recruitment arm and education program geared towards American youth. With my plan, they'll become a true auxiliary that pays civilian mariners to handle cable laying, salvage, towing, icebreaking and buoy tending. There's no reason for our coast guard to build these niche-role vessels, let alone run them full time, if they're hardly ever needed.

Auxiliary Support:

Whenever one is warranted, the U.S. Coast Guard shall call upon local mariners to fulfill these roles. Our navy already has its USMM seafaring fleet as their auxiliary. While privateers rely on explorers, sailors will contact merchant mariners instead.

Leadership

DOD Membership:

My plan places the CBP as a permanent fourth branch in the U.S. Department of Defense. No longer shall they transfer to the Dept. of Homeland Security during peacetime! When major wars break out, the U.S. Coast Guard goes from its standard paramilitary loadouts to military-grade firepower and electronics packages. This grants cutters the ability to engage modern enemy warships, submarines and aircraft threatening our coastlines. Allied convoys and cruise ships need better coverage!

CHAPTER TEN

Managing Arsenals

<u>Quadrant 2:5</u>

Listed below is this chapter's section directory. Topics are grouped together in subsections labeled by underlined bullets. Any further subdivision of information is organized into verses marked by bolded bullets.

Overview

Munitions

Regular Personnel:

Cast polymer stocks, rubber grips, milled barrels and stamped steel should be the only materials used. Avoid manufacturing expensive aluminum parts! To save money, only issue military personnel one primary weapon without customized modifications.

Special Loadouts:

Snipers operating behind enemy lines require suppressed pistols. This explains why they carry secondary armaments. Tank crews traded their pistols for M3 Grease Guns. Commandos enjoy Knight's Armament SOPMOD loadouts, such as reflex sights, lasers, etc. Apart from SWAT, most policemen pay for their firearms out of pocket.

Ammo Caches

Military Ammunition:

Shotgun: .410 > 20ga > 12ga

Carbine: 4.5mm > 5.45 > 5.56

Assault: .30 Car > 6.5G > 6.8 SPC

Battle: .303 > 7.5 GP > 7.62 NATO

MMG: 7.92 > .30-06 > 7.62 NATO

Anti-material: BMG > API > SLAP

Sidearm: 7.65 > 9mm > 10mm

Police Ammunition:

Shotgun: .410 > 20-gauge > 12-gauge

MP: .17 HMR > .22 Short > .25 ACP

PDW: .32 Auto > .380 ACP > .38 Super

SMG: 4.6mm > 5.7mm > 6.5mm

Sniper: .30-06 > .300 MAG > .338 Lapula

Compact: .41 SPC > .45cal > .40cal

SC Pistol: .41 SPC > .44 US > .45cal

Hunting Rounds:

Hunting Rifle: .338 Norma > .358 Magnum > .375 H-H (ex: hunters)

Stopper Rifle: .404 > .416 > .45-70 Government (ex: tour guides)

Park Sidearm: .38 Long > .38 Special > .357 MAG (ex: rangers)

Zoo Sidearm: .44 MAG > .454 Casull > .460 (ex: zoo security)

Ocean Sidearm: .475 > .480 > .500 (ex: U.S. Sea Marshals)

Small Arms Inventory

Includes all police, park rangers and military branches.

Browning M2A1 HMG: $14,000 each

Army tanks, cavalry vehicles and coast guard vessels station "Ma Deuces" in barbettes to fire anti-material rounds at vehicles. Browning manufactures all AP-tipped, .50cal BMG.

U.S. Ordinance M240B MMG: $6,600 each

Army vehicles and USCG boats fire general-purpose machine guns (MMGs) at enemy personnel and soft targets. Federal Premium supplies "Bravos" 7.62mm NATO in FMJ.

Ohio Ordinance M249 LMG: $3,000 each

U.S. military modifies BARs as light machine guns (LMGs) to offer troops an affordable SAW platform. Kramer Industries produces 6.8 x 45mm Kramer ammunition in FMJ.

Colt M16A4/M203 Assault Rifle: $1,800 each

Grenadiers lob M203 grenades into windowsills from outdoor positions to defend squads of infantry as they enter buildings. Load Kramer Industries 6.8 x 45mm in FMJ.

Colt M4A1/KEY Carbine: $600-1,000 each

CQB assault rifle capable of mounting fighting knives as bayonets. Corporals attach Knight's Armament Masterkey shotgun attachments to breach doors for fireteams.

Springfield Armory M1A DMR: $1,850 each

Sniper teams can opt for designated marksmen rifles (DMRs) instead of bolt-action rifles in urban combat environments with silencers. Issue Federal 7.62 NATO in FMJ.

Winchester XPR Safari: $750 each

Anti-material snipers conduct operations to destroy vehicles or dispose of explosive ordinance. Weapons are bolt-action, .50cals equipped with 12x scopes and bipods. Browning's SLAP rounds contain tungsten sabots lacking depleted uranium or RDX.

Winchester XPR Sporter: $650 each

Correctional officers supervise prison yards and perimeters in guard towers. Models come standard with 10x scopes and bipods. Rifles are fed .30-06 Springfield in JHP.

Winchester XPR Compact: $550 each

SWAT fields snipers in windowsills or on rooftops during HRT missions. They stabilize a compact rifle outfitted with 8x scopes and bipods. Winchester's .300 MAG in JHP penetrates windows and body armor with ease. Cross breezes won't be an issue!

SDS MAC-11 MP: $350 each

Secret Service guarding presidents and U.S. Marshals performing witness protection conceal subcompact machine pistols with folding butt stocks. Colt's .25 ACP in SJHP.

SDS MAC-10 PDW: $400 each

Correctional officers (COs) provide overwatch while chain gangs labor outdoors at state park systems with personal defense weapons (PDWs). Colt's .38 Super in HP.

IWI Uzi SMG: $900 each

SWAT operators perform raids with silenced submachine guns (SMGs). CBJ Tech's 6.5mm CBJ in JHP boosts penetration and stopping power without overpenetration.

Savage 775 Shotgun: $200 each

Masterkeys swap Remington 830s for 775s on M4A1s. Remington's Gun Club shells.

Stevens 320 Shotgun: $250 each

COs' riot guns! MK Ballistics manufactures their 12ga., non-lethal, bean bag rounds.

Stevens 124 Shotgun: $300 each

SWAT operatives breach doors with 124s. Remington's Gun Club in 12ga. magnum.

RemArms R1 Hunter: $200-600 each

Military officers' sidearm ordered in bulk to drive down costs to $200. Commandos' silenced versions cost $600. Federal Premium supplies 10mm American Eagle in FMJ.

RemArms R1 Limited: $180 each

Compact pistol for paramilitary raids. Bulk purchase discount. S&W's 40cal in JHP.

RemArms R1 Ultralight: $160 each

Police subcompact. Bulk purchase discount. Colt Manufacturing's .45cal ACP in HP.

S&W 686 Plus: $300 each

Park rangers' 6-shot revolvers have full-sized 6" barrels. S&W's .357 MAG in JHP.

S&W 460V: $350 each

Zoo patrols prevent rampages with their 5-shot, short magnums. S&W .460 in JHP.

S&W 500 HI VIZ: $400 each

Sea marshals prevent marine attacks. 5-shot snub revolvers. S&W .500 MAG in JHP.

Henry H010 Stopper: $800 each

Zoo crisis. Fires Pneu-Dart tranquilizer rounds or Hornady .470 Nitro Express in JHP.

Henry Big Boy X Stopper: $700 each

Park rangers. Unleashes Pneu-Dart tranquilizers or Hornady .375 H&H MAG in JHP.

Guided Ammunition

LGM-30G Minuteman IV: $1.5 million each

1,500-mile MIRV ABMs for ballistic defense. Major Kong's hologram and sounds!

UGM-133 Trident III: $1.2 million each

800-mile MIRV ABMs onboard boomer subs. Major Kong's hologram and sounds!

Raytheon XGM-51 Tomahawk: $1 million each

Block Vs, but HMX lets them dump half their girth. Outcompetes BrahMos-II's range.

Raytheon XGM-84 Harpoon: $700,000 each

Block IIs, but twice as skinny and filled with HMX. U (sub), A (jet) or R (ship) options.

Raytheon AGM-88G HARM: $450,000 each

AARGM-ER models are now half as wide due to HMX. For fighter jets' SEAD missions.

Raytheon AIM-54 Phoenix: $250,000 each

AIM-54Cs become much thinner thanks to HMX. Replaces Sea Sparrows on warships.

Raytheon AIM-120C AMRAAM: $225,000 each

AIM-120Cs made slender by HMX. Medium-ranged, radar-guided, air-to-air missiles.

Raytheon AIM-9X Sidewinder: $200,000 each

AIM-9Xs streamlined by using HMX. Short-ranged, heat-seeking, air-to-air missiles.

Raytheon AGM-114R Hellfire II: $65,000 each

Romeo blocks, but narrower thanks to HMX. Laser-guided, anti-tank missiles.

Alliant Techsystems Mk-48 Lancer: $800,000 each

My "B" blocks are slimmer by loading HMX. TOW-guided torpedoes for submarines.

Alliant Techsystems Mk-54 LHT: $800,000 each

LHT models opt for HMX making them skinnier. TOW-guided torpedoes for warships.

Alliant Techsystems BLU-82 Daisy Cutter: $75,000 each

GPS-guided, bunker busters are ½ the size, packed full of HMX and open parachutes.

Alliant Techsystems Mk-83 JDAM: $40,000 each

GPS-guided, 2,000lb bombs stuffed with HMX. A second version replaces GBU-28s!

Military Service Uniforms

Design

Velcro Pockets:

Rear trouser pockets store wallets and coin bags. Front pockets are for cell phones and key chains. Watch pockets anchor wallet chains. Blouse pockets harbor training whistles and stopwatches. Coat pockets can conceal documents or business cards. Fatigues stash primary mags in blouse pockets and secondary clips in cargo pockets.

Shoulder Flaps:

Buttoned shoulder flaps can attach ghillie suits, sleeveless trench coats, rain ponchos and aiguilette whips. Sleeves hold enlistees' chevrons. Ditch those backwards flags! Servicemen always place carry straps on their right and awards to the left during presentation. For tuffs, "macaroni" was for 18th century uniforms and as patches displaying ranks on Civil War uniforms. Adapt Pershing's collar on all dress uniforms.

Skater Belts:

Webbed belts prevent blouses from shifting about and accommodate a hostler, baton, flashlight or knife. Straps course through shoulder flaps allowing a rifle to be slung along their backside if necessary. Dress uniforms equip machete swords for military weddings or 21-gun salutes. Each instructor and camp commandant only wear one shoulder-mounted whip at a time. Boot camp sergeants are jr. NCOs. Cornets/ensigns are their seniors, both wearing lanyards. At academies, commanders are basic instructors and colonels serve as camp commandants over the entire academy adorned by aiguillettes.

Decor

Insignia Pins:

Collars on dress shirts display pins with officer ranks or enlistees' branch insignia. Place U.S. eagle pins above personnel's last names on their right. Wear awards during ceremonies and ribbons on dress uniforms on the left. Peaked caps, campaign covers, digger hats and side caps showcase their branch's seal. U.S. and branch acronyms are clearly visible. Forge pins out of white brass and scrambled eggs from yellow brass.

Service Stripes:

Replace our service branches' arm stripping with more streamlined cuff lacing. Study the British RAF and Royal Navy's sleave designs. Remodeled designs accordingly. It needs to be easy to understand and memorize without being hard on one's eyes.

Apparel

ROTC Academies:

Green on all USA/USMC/USAF pilot jumpers. Navy and coast guardsmen wear grey coveralls. Air crews sport leather jackets, bomber caps, Aviators and helmets. Parade uniforms come in grey (USA), royal blue (USAF) and navy blue (USN/USMC/USCG).

Dress Uniforms:

Men's blues don dress coats and slacks. Women's dress graces us with full-length skirts, blouses and slippers. Issue female USN/USCG drill instructors pillboxes; the rest wear Aussie digger hats. Male drill instructors keep their campaign covers. Ditch PTs belts outright. Switch between shorts or tracksuits depending on the weather.

Headgear Items:

Men's dress implements peaked caps. Naval outfits issue men Dixie caps and women pillboxes. The other branches' female dress entails giving enlistees side caps and officers forage caps. Our commandos wear berets on service uniforms regardless of gender. Make black represent SEALs, green Green Berets and maroon PJ Rangers. For fatigues, enlistees wear helmets, commandos boonie hats and officers patrol caps.

Branches

U.S. Army:

The Honor Guard's blue dress (white-tie), service blue (black-tie) and service green (informal). Use current Scorpion woodland (fatigues) and ranger green PTs (training).

Marine Corps:

Blue-white dress (white-tie) with white slacks, blues (black-tie) with red side striping, service green (informal), MARPAT woodland (fatigues) and olive green PTs (training).

U.S. Air Force:

Command dress (white-tie), band (black-tie) and service blues (informal). Redesign improved, greyer versions of the ABU woodland (fatigues). Make PTs (training) grey.

U.S. Navy:

Dress whites (white-tie), blues (black-tie) and khakis (informal). Design superior, less purple Blueberries (fatigues) and navy blue PTs (training). Do the same to the SEAL's Avocado woodland. Supplies of arctic Ice Cream must be shared by other branches.

Coast Guard:

Maintain dress whites (white-tie), blues (black-tie), service blues (business informal) and ODUs (fatigues). Improve PTs (training) by making them baby blue, not grey.

Review

Armories

Kevlar Protection:

Aviation crews wear flak jackets (Level I). Undercover concealed vests (Level IIA) accommodate Level IIIa plate inserts. SWAT operatives add Level III plates to ballistic patrol vests (Level II). Military plate carriers (Level IIIA) house Level IV ceramic tiles.

Service Outfits:

Stockpile American Apparel underwear, Propper uniforms and Frye boots for the military. Issue police forces Blauer uniforms, DuPont Kevlar vests, Nomex balaclavas, Maglite flashlights, Mace S.I. pepper spray, Peerless handcuffs and walkie-talkies.

Armament

Explosive Ordinance:

Make Raytheon's missiles half the size by shoving HMX in them so everything fits in a FIM-92 launcher! Stingers should cost $20,000. M72 recoilless sabots run $6,000. Try Mohawk Electrical Systems' claymore mines, door charges and satchel explosives.

Grenade Launchers:

MK19 grenade launchers built by General Dynamics fire 40mm rounds and set you back $20,000. Hawk MM-1 barbettes atop of SWAT APCs fire tear gas during riots. M67 hand grenades cost $45. Stockpile Orbital ATK flashbangs and smoke grenades.

Weapons Modifications:

Ka-Bar Mk. 2 fighting knives also double as bayonets! Blades, rubber handles and leather holsters are all matte black. Honor guards' ceremonial M14s mount parade bayonets. Knights Armament offers commandos and SWAT operatives SOPMOD. Infantry rely on Newcon's M22 binoculars and Elbit Systems' PVS-14 night vision goggles (NVGs).

Non-lethal Compliance:

Police use Axon tasers, MK Ballistics bean bag shells, Atlas International tear gas grenades (40mm), Paulson Manufacturing riot shields and Monadnock nightsticks. Stun guns are obsolete electroshock weapons only effective at point blank range.

CHAPTER ELEVEN

Tonnage Creep Pact

Quadrant 3:1

Listed below is this chapter's section directory. Topics are grouped together in subsections labeled by underlined bullets. Any further subdivision of information is organized into verses marked by bolded bullets.

Overview

Militaries

Tonnage Creep:

Regional powers are struggling to build blue-water fleets. Great powers also fight to maintain theirs due to growing ship sizes. Destroyers are already too large to do their original job: eliminate torpedo boats and submarines! The best option is to cap size ranges and encourage smaller nations to build brown-water fleets. Green-water, merchant marine fleets can stretch the oceangoing capabilities of these navies. This gives them the ability to perform salvage missions, search and rescue operations, anti-piracy endeavors, embassy work and assist other allied forces already in battle.

Power Ratings:

There are many countries trying to manage too many branches than they should. If they're not capable of justifying two or more three-stars during peacetime capable of leading corps, fleets or wings: Then consolidate said branches down! The United States didn't even split its own air force off of its regular army until after WWII ended!

Flexible Branches:

Landlocked armies field boats and fighter jets if they lack an air force. Giving soldiers, marines, sailors and privateers helicopters eliminates the need for internal joint commands. Green Berets operate rigid, rubber inflatable rafts for river operations. One service branch asking another for assistance doesn't require a joint command.

Militias

Civilian Auxiliaries:

Each branch has their standing (actives), militia (reserve) and auxiliary (contractors). Historically, auxiliaries were other countries' forces grafted under someone else's command. Now, they're civilian contractors! They'll move personnel to air bases, supply fleets and unload combat engineering vehicles at bases. Explorers assist the USCG by performing offshore maintenance along American shoreline instillations.

Naval Realignment

Rename current watercraft with the chart below. Tonnages are max deep load displacements in short tons, not standard displacement or long tonnage.

Blue Water

Surface Combatants:

above 28,000 tons: Fast Battleship (*Military Museum Rental*)

10,000 to 28,000 tons: Large Cruiser (*Obsolete after Cold War*)

4,000 to 10,000 tons: Guided Cruiser (*Cold War to Current*)

2,000 to 4,000 tons: Guided Destroyer (*Cold War to Current*)

1,000 to 2,000 tons: Guided Frigate (*Cold War to Current*)

under 1,000 tons: Guided Corvette (Cold War *to* Current)

Modern Submarines:

above 4,000 tons: Cruiser Submarine (*Obsolete after WWII*)

above 2,000 tons: Fleet Submarine (*Obsolete after WWII*)

2,000 to 4,000 tons: Ballistic Defense Sub (*Cold War to Current*)

1,000 to 2,000 tons: Hunter-killer (*Cold War to Current*)

under 1,000 tons: Mine Warfare (*Cold War to Current*)

50 to 500 tons: Missile Boat (*Cold War to Current*)

Brown Water

Coastal Defense Craft:

under 500 tons: Offshore Patrol

50 to 100 tons: Inshore Patrol

20 to 50 tons: Fast Patrol Boat

10 to 20 tons: Offshore Lifeboat

under 10 tons: Inshore Lifeboat

500 to 1,000 tons: Coastal Sub

200 to 500 tons: Minelayer Sub

under 150 tons: Midget Sub

under 20 tons: Wet Sub (DPV)

under 10 tons: ROV Drone

Air-independent propulsion (AIP) makes submarine engines quieter.

Midget subs target hostiles while submersibles perform MCMV.

Peacetime Minimums

United Nations

Unified Command Plan: UCP

United Nations supplanted the WWI League of Nations. Prior to UCP's creation, we had Rainbows. These color-coordinated plans split Earth into five army regions. Tom Clancy's *Rainbow Six* was a global anti-terrorist group inspired by this plan. After WWII, they were superseded by eight unified combatant commands, aka our UCCs! Albeit, we only need seven. Near space's ABM grid is split amongst the existing seven.

Security Council

Great Powers: (4 branches)

Regular air force, blue-water navy, army and CBP commission. One air division, naval squadron, marine division, army corps, coast guard division and border patrol agency per standing and reserve. Leader of the Free World doubles as UCP's Supreme Commander of the Allied Powers, aka SCAP! Other heads of government from allied great powers are appointed as supreme allied commanders to lead wartime theatres.

Regional Powers: (3 branches)

Green-water navy, regular army and CBP commission. One naval squadron, marine division, army corps, coast guard division and border patrol agency per standing and reserve. Regional heads of government serve as combatant commanders, aka CCDRs. UCP army regions are unified combatant commands (CCMDs). They shall manage resistance efforts on behalf of the middle powers orchestrated at continental levels!

Middle Powers: (2 branches)

Regular army and CBP commission. One army corps, coast guard division and border patrol agency per standing and reserve. Some countries commission wartime four-star officers as chiefs of defense (CHODs). Other might opt for a civilian defense minister. These commanders-in-chief (CNCs) organize sub-unified commands as subordinated commanders (SCDRs) as subordinated commanders (SCDRs) protecting small powers.

Small Powers: (1 branch)

Irregular military with one border patrol agency, coast guard division and national police precinct per standing and reserve. CBP commissioners serve as CHODs. Nations should remain neutral. Territories receive protection from their mother countries.

Reorganized Militia

Definement

Organized militias include countries' national guards or irregular police forces.

National guards are militias staffed by part-time civilians called <u>active reserves</u>.

Irregular militaries lack a true <u>standing army</u>, or full-time professional troops.

Irregulars enact a self-defense force or CBP branch as their <u>irregular military</u>.

Draft pools from irregular militaries are always referred to as <u>reserve militia</u>.

Draft pools of regular militaries are often nicknamed <u>unorganized reserves</u>.

Both groups aren't standing or part-time. They're just our <u>inactive reserves</u>.

Auxiliaries include contracted civilian volunteers, aka the <u>select militias</u>.

They're only called if they're needed, hence the term <u>select reserves</u>.

Contracting them reduces the vehicles we purchase during major wars.

Contractors aren't militiamen and sell their products to our militaries.

JROTC trains our enlisted men and the ROTC educated future officers.

National Guard

Space Guard: Space National Guard manages guardian reservists (USSF).

Air Guard: Air National Guard serves as our country's air guard (USAF).

Home Guard: Army National Guard is the heartland's home guard (USA).

Border Guard: Marine National Guard harbors marine reservists (USMC).

Naval Guard: Naval National Guard is our military's naval guard (USN).

Coast Guard: USCG Reserve is the coast guard's reserve force (USCG).

Auxiliaries

Civil Air Patrol: Civilian pilots assist our air force's logistics (USAF).

MARS Radio: Coordinates contractors and civilian truckers (USA).

Merchant Marine: Seafarers resupply our naval fleets (USN).

Explorers: Mariners perform offshore maintenance (USCG).

Review

Defense

Air Dominance:

CBP divisions of small powers must focus on defending their own country and no one else. All they must build is combatant aircraft. Bulking up on fighter jets holds top priority over anything. Doing so helps small powers wield up to half of our air force's fighting strength! If everyone else did so too, middle powers would hit 2/3rds and regional powers 75% of the USAF's combat ability! During peacetime, they can roll unnecessary aircraft into boneyards, cannibalize unsalvageable husks for parts or sell excess units through lend-lease to pay off war debts. Air supremacy must come first!

Internal Security:

Middle powers are usually landlocked states, but their armies still contain numerous air regiments and boat battalions. Having less land to protect makes covering said territory with SSM, SAM and CISW batteries affordable. What they lack in tanks is compensated by attack drones. Regional powers are coastal nations capable of buildings navies with at least one brown-water fleet. Oceangoing vessels require merchant mariners to extend their endurance, meaning they're not truly green-water like those supply ships. Blue-water navies can circumnavigate the World indefinitely.

Security

Nuclear Treaties:

Current nuclear treaties prevent us from converting nuclear arsenals to affordable, anti-ballistic missiles (ABMs) systems and performing weapons testing. Heads of government need to reach an agreement and convince the United Nations to ratify new amendments to existing legislation. ABM prototypes are allowed to successfully intercept one ballistic missile in three of Earth's atmospheric layers: Mesosphere, thermosphere and exosphere. Afterwards, these product lines and their brands are barred from any future testing. UN weapons inspectors record the evidence before any silo can begin embarking on these projects and send it to the public to witness.

CHAPTER TWELVE

Joint Command Plans

Quadrant 3:2

Listed below is this chapter's section directory. Topics are grouped together in subsections labeled by underlined bullets. Any further subdivision of information is organized into verses marked by bolded bullets.

Overview

Free World

Military Coalitions:

Modern military alliances have an overly-complicated and overengineered system of permanent joint commands. Most defense ministers are too stressed-out to manage more than their own country's defense forces. U.S. presidents need to step up as our commanders-in-chief and coordinate future coalitions between major NATO allies! Other allied heads of government need to do the same for their defense chiefs too!

Multinational Task Forces:

Pershing's American Expeditionary Force (AEF) was the first U.S. campaign to pioneer this history-making principle by not subordinating his combatants within existing French formations. Militaries can coordinate their standing forces across plural theatres and army regions, aka fronts. Devastated allied units can opt to remain in separate commands and assist us as our nonorganic detachments. Smaller, local defense forces fulfill their role according to my UCP models, sometimes as auxiliaries.

U.S. Military

Civilian Leadership:

Citizens without military experience were sometimes elected as military secretaries, which placed immense stress on the Joint Chiefs of Staff. Enact requirements stating only the top-retired, branch personnel available at our disposal are allowed to be appointed as defense ministers, secretaries, adjutants and aides. Redefine job duties to include leading command-level administrations, wearing suits and carrying batons.

Joint Commands:

My next chapter's strategies utilize this book's military inventory in a manner forever preventing the need to maintain joint commands between our allies, let alone service branches. Names from pre-existing organizations have been repurposed to represent future wartime commands, most of which remain deactivated during peacetime.

Unified Command Plan

NATO Alliance

Heads of Government:

UCP is a global contingency operation. Normally, eight regions were given to four-star (NATO OF9) officers. Giving the planetary seven ABM and ASAT capabilities renders Space Command unnecessary. U.S. presidents are SCAPs and great powers SACs. Regional powers operate the remaining UCCs. Middle powers can lead sub-unified commands. Combined organizations involve two or more countries' defenses.

Unified Combatant Commands:

Wartime theatres can encompass plural regions, but aren't always that big. During war, regions contain frontlines across no-man's land. For example: The Western Front, not to be confused with Russian army groups called fronts. Seven regions have been dubbed unified combatant commands (UCCs) covering North America, South America, Europe/Siberia, Africa, Middle East, Mainland Asia and Australia/Oceania.

The Pentagon

Chiefs of Defense:

Maps sent to defense ministers have the option of toggling between allied coalitions' advances and their countries' miliary movements across the known World. Doing so lets them devise plans for their service branches too. Branch secretaries are given their own versions only showing their branches' commands to avoid any confusion.

Joint Chiefs of Staff:

U.S. Presidents relay orders to defense chiefs (CHODs). Branch secretaries appoint adjutants and aides-de-camp to abolish the roles of six, five and four-star officers forever. JCS membership includes CHODs appointed as chairmen (unisex title), and three branch secretaries. Space Legion commandants, USMC commandants, CBP commissioners, National Guard chiefs and CIA directors visit them as guest advisors.

U.S. STRATCOM:

Once nuclear treaties ratify amendments allowing nuclear ABMs, redesign ICBMs as affordable anti-ballistic missiles designed to shoot down oncoming nukes in near space. Doing so prevents nuclear fallout! USAF Minuteman IV and USN Trident III ICBMs contain multiple warheads (MIRVs). CIA satellites guide GPS systems in place of traditional stellar navigation. Space Legion guardians operate mission control.

HEADCOMs

Chiefs of Staff:

HEADCOM is short for headquarters command, inspired by USAF's historic Air Force District of Washington (AFDW). They serve as branch administrations. Two-star (OF-7) general officers in the form of divisionnaires and superintendents run these agencies. These senior advisors ride aboard staff cars, ideally ISVs, to inspect regional headquarters bases. Anything smaller than divisions double as wartime formations.

Grand Marshals:

Although no seven-star rank is acknowledged by the Free World, our defense chiefs would be their equivalent. North Korea awarded its founder Kim Il-Sung and his son Kim Jong-Il taewonsu, the latter greater in seniority. Before communism forced the Republic of China's relocation to Taiwan, three people held the title dàyuánshuài. To prevent shoguns from usurping power, emperors adorned themselves as dai-gensui. Genarlissimos and their naval equivalent admiralissimos formed military juntas. China's communist party is a regime while North Korea's dictator is their strongman.

Special Grades:

Admiral of the Navy Dewey defeated Spain's Armada during the Spanish-American War! General of the Armies Pershing, aka Blackjack, led the American Expeditionary Force during the Battle of Argonne Forest, which ended the Great War! He was the first to be promoted to grand marshal during his lifetime. George Washington was awarded this rank in the '70s and remains senior to all others bearing this rank. Ulysses S. Grant was awarded it in 2022 and became the third to hold such a title.

MAJCOMs

Major Commands:

MAJCOMs remain inactive during peacetime. Adjutants lead districts, army groups and combined fleets dressed in business informal while carrying batons The latter formation was named after Imperial Japan's Combined Fleet. The British Grand Fleet, German High Seas Fleet and U.S. Great White Fleet were prime examples in military history. Combined fleets and merchant marine fleets funnel into their regular navies.

TACCOMs

Tactical Commands:

Aides-de-camp, aka camp "aides," drive four-star commands during major wars. Formations include tactical air forces, field armies and standing "readiness" fleets. TACCOMs are numbered formations while everything else above them is spelled out, or named. For example, Twelfth U.S. Army Group vs. the U.S. 1st Army (field army).

American Diplomacy

Convocations

Awards Ceremonies:

Congressional Medals of Honor require approval from Congress. The president bestows them to worthy personnel. Certain awards not monopolized by service branches can be given to defense ministers by the POTUS. Ministers commemorate secretaries with their service branch's honors. Each superior does the same towards one's subordinates. For example: Secretary > adjutant > aide-de-camp > general, etc.

Addressing Troops:

Armed forces personnel are troops, not warriors. Troops are professionals who serve the people while warrior castes did the opposite to peasant subjects. We the People do not want to be the inferiors of our armed forces personnel! Special forces are comprised of commandos, space forces guardians, air forces airmen, armies soldiers, navies sailors, marines the marines, coast guards privateers and border patrol agents.

Force Multipliers:

Ship crewmembers are seamen regardless if they're military personnel. Civilians, such as those in the U.S. Merchant Marine fleet, include oceangoing seafarers and domestic mariners. American citizens must pledge allegiance to the American flag and honor our national anthem. Those who don't witness their citizenship revoked!

Consulates

U.S. Embassies:

We commission five kinds of diplomats, four of which can host delegations. The secretary of state superintends all diplomatic missions. An ambassador-at-large represents us in the UN General Assembly. Every U.S. embassy has one ambassador assisted by several emissaries. Envoys are responsible for delivering messages. Attaché includes civilian Peace Corps volunteers and the Marine Corps as guards.

United Nations:

Member states supply the UN with their own domestic brands of helicopters. While our military mass produces Bell models to save money, we'll still maintain Sikorsky Blackhawk transports and Boeing Chinook cargo choppers to supply or evacuate landlocked U.S. embassies. Peacekeepers cross into sovereign states and can establish temporary legates tasked with granting American tourists in hostile lands asylum.

Review

Maritime

Leasing Battleships:

During the Korean War, Douglas McArthur controlled North Korea entirely until China decided to deploy millions of its soldiers. Grey Ghost (USS Iowa) single-handedly stopped the Chinese Army from pursuing retreating U.S. marines! Fast battleships serving as nonorganic naval elements could deter millions of infantrymen! Positions: Wisconsin (Hong Kong), Iowa (Taiwan), New Jersey (N/S Korea) and Missouri (Israel).

Naval Aviation Exhibits:

Numerous roles exist for future military museums. F-35s serve as targeting units for three other air exhibits. Their supercomputers fire their ordinance for them since they lack the proper electronics to fire their own weapon systems. F-14s carry Phoenix missiles intended to down supersonic bombers armed with cruise missiles and Iranian Tomcats. F/A-18s are outfitted with ASW torpedoes and ant-ship missiles. USMC bases scramble AV-8B Harrier IIs to fire rockets at oncoming ground forces.

Terrestrial

USAF Air Shows:

Unfortunately, only one F-111 exists outside Australia located in Hawaii. Only 20 SR-71 Blackbirds, four airworthy F-177s and a pair of RAH-66s exist today. However, placing stealth and bomber aircraft in future exhibits remains a viable option. F-22s target for fighter jets and other rentals. Bombers drop cluster munitions over enemy infantrymen. B-1s represent daytime, B-2s nighttime. A-10s supplant these two in mountainous regions opting to mount Hydra rockets instead of JDAMs. The combat radius of B-52s lets them fire nuclear cruise missiles deep into enemy-held territory.

Army Museums:

Retired AH-64s guard army outposts loaded with rockets. Abrams tanks, Bradley IFVs, and M270s modified to shoot det cord escort civilian convoys in war-torn areas.

CHAPTER THIRTEEN

Military Organization

Quadrant 3:3

Listed below is this chapter's section directory. Topics are grouped together in subsections labeled by underlined bullets. Any further subdivision of information is organized into verses marked by bolded bullets.

Overview

Operations

Amphibious Supply:

During major wars, the Merchant Marine mass produce Victory ships. These JSS units supply our fleets and double as barracks ships during landings. Restrict exports to convoy routes escorted by helicopters launched from guided frigates. Hunter-killer submarines conduct offensive operations beforehand. Light radio lets them transmit Morse code messages via laser beams. Signals are sped-up to create blue lasers behind them and slowed-down by HAM radio operators to generate text messages!

Ground Initiatives:

IFVs fulfill the role of light tanks for amphibious landings and jungle conditions. MBTs are restricted to upland countryside and urban environments. Between missions, semis haul tanks to save fuel. Rail is the most efficient supply method stateside. Bases in warzones send supply trucks in nocturnal convoys escorted by armored vehicles.

Air Supremacy:

Landing gear should factor in runways that are shorter, crumbling or made of dirt. Turbojets are solely for trainer aircraft, turboprops drones, turboshafts helicopters and turbofans everything else. Internal weapons bays were designed in an era where unguided ordinance was dropped all at once. External pylons individually release guided, miniature, C4-filled munitions with less moving parts. Any perceived lack in stealth is rectified by radar-absorbent paint, passive radar, ECMs and Giraffe tactics.

Fortifications

Constructing Bases:

Overseas construction should entail highly-affordable and available prefabricated parts capable of folding down to smaller sizes. Make everything compact utilizing the lightest possible materials, Embrace the art of making sandbags! Bases resemble vehicle and fuel depots. Give them armor, artillery, barracks, fuel and warehouses.

Naval Strategies

Grand Tactics

Drones: MPA units patrol naval bases. CAS drones target enemy drone teams.
Bases: F-20s establish air supremacy and target enemy surface ships for cruisers.
Boomers: Boomers air blast enemy nukes in near space and target spy satellites.
Hunters: Subs target enemy ships for surface vessels and interdict supply convoys.
Auxiliaries: Resupply the U.S. Navy and export civilian products internationally.
Convoys: Guided frigates prevent piracy along convoys with their helicopters.
Destroyers: Eliminate watercraft, deploy MCMVs and support USMC Raiders.
Cruisers: Coordinates boomers, fires TLAMs at MLRS/ships and offers NGFS.
Battleships: Museum rentals provide shore bombardment and JSS support.
Carriers: F-20s establish air superiority and launch preemptive SEAD missions.
SDVs: Hunter-killer subs insert SEAL Teams to perform nocturnal scouting.
MCMV: Proteus submersibles can double as a minehunter and minesweeper.
LHDs: Coordinate LCUs and launch LCMs. AH-1Ws escort their UH-1N medivacs.
LCUs: Fires rockets to protect IFVs. Vehicles deploy infantry to clear buildings.
JSSs: Barracks ships create human bucket brigades to reinforce LHD amphibs.
STABs: USMC Raiders travel upriver to eliminate any remaining inland threats.
LCMs: Delivers reinforcements and supplies to the Raiders' makeshift camps.

Major Tactics

Bases: Establish temporary overseas bases to station more fighters and LCUs.
Tenders: Victory ships serve as tenders of LCU flotillas sailing across the sea.
Flotillas: Guided frigates protect these convoys with their ASW helicopters.
Fighters: HARMs disable enemy SAM sites. JDAMs destroy coastal air bases.
HELOs: Super Cobras perform ASW patrols. Hueys resupply U.S. embassies.
SSMs: TLAM cruise missiles outrange enemy coastal MLRS and strike buildings.
Torpedoes: Mk-48s are given to submarines. Surface vessels equip Mk-50 pods.

Minor Tactics

Morse Code: All service branches carry flashlights and mirrors during rescues.
Light Radio: Subs convert laser pings into Morse code and play them on radios.
Electronics: Aegis, radar, thermal imaging, radio, SONAR, light radio and GPS.
Countermeasures: ECM pods, chaff, flares, torpedo decoys and smokescreens.
Camo: Paint watercraft and aircraft silver. Ground assets don M81 Woodland.

Military Campaigns

U.S. Air Force

ABMs: USAF satellites assist Minutemen IVs in destroying nukes in near space.
Drones: AWAC units patrol bases. CAS drones neutralize enemy drone teams.
Fighters: F-20s guard bases. F-16s achieve air supremacy before guiding F-15s.
Interdiction: F-15s are tasked with SEAD operations and DAS bombing raids.
Airdrops: C-130s drop Daisy Cutters over bunkers and resupply combatants.
HALOs: PJs HALO jump out of Starlifters to rescue POWs. C-141s supply bases.
HELOs: Super Cobras escort Huey gunships tasked with extracting PJ Rangers.
Tankers: KC-135s fly behind enemy lines to extend everyone's combat radius.
Camo: Paint all aircraft dark grey and give ground vehicles M81 Woodland.

U.S. Army

Drones: AGS units patrol army bases. CAS drones target enemy drone teams.
Bases: MLRS targets enemy tanks and artillery. Mortar carriers repel infantry.
Camps: SPGs conduct artillery strikes for tanks. Grenade carriers defend them.
TFAs: Rugged terrain demands towed artillery. Mountains require HELO drops.
HALOs: Green Berets HALO jump behind enemy lines to secure landlocked rivers.
HELOs: Super Cobras escort Huey gunships while they extract the Green Berets.
MBTs: Universal tanks eliminate outdoor threats before blockading city streets.
Airdrops: C-130s drop Daisy Cutters over bunkers and resupply our combatants.
Logistics: Cargo planes supply bases. Trucks reinforce and medivac wounded.
Camo: Paint all aircraft dark grey. Vehicles and artillery pieces are light tan.

Army Tactics

Group: Adjutants organize groups tasked with liberating subcontinents.
Field: Aides-de-camp lead field armies ending occupation of countries.
Corps: Generals (three-star) deploy corps to free entire regions of nations.
Division: Divisionnaires push divisions to break enemy lines in provinces.
Brigade: Brigadiers establish MOB bases focused on district-level planning.
Battalion: Colonels operate FOB bases responsible for liberating cities.
Company: Commanders set up campsites outside bases called outposts.
Platoon: Cornets are shift managers at camps and coordinate missions.
Squad: Sergeants lead squads deployed in IFVs to secure city streets.
Team: Corporals move fireteams through buildings to clear out rooms.

Brigade System

Command: Group and field armies are the largest commands officers can manage.
Formation: Corps and divisions form major battle formations during world wars.
Unit: Brigades and battalions are garrisoned units stationed at allied operating bases.
Subunit: Companies and platoons are subcategories of the units dubbed subunits.
Element: Full squads and fireteams are designated as subordinated elements.
Fire and Movement: Tage teams of battle buddies fulfill fire and movement.

A corps has enough supply lines to operate independently and indefinitely.

Legions are the smallest formation capable of leading a military campaign.

Operating Systems

MOBs: Main Operating Bases. Corps-level headquarters, aka overseas HQs.
FOBs: Forward Operating Bases. Division-level bases; smaller wartime bases.
FOSs: Forward Operating Sites. Brigade-level camps, aka arty outposts.
CSLs: Cooperative Security Locations. Battalion outposts orbiting FOBs.

Combat Engineering

Fencing: Gabions serve as perimeter fencing topped with razor wire.
Towers: Prefab towers out of chain link fencing anchored by cinderblocks.
Pillboxes: Sandbags form security checkpoints for machine gun nests.
Warehouses: Sheet metal unfolds to harbor supplies and fuel tanks.
Garages: Camo netting tents shroud army vehicles from enemy arty.
Hangers: Cinderblock creates hardened hangers over army aircraft.
Barracks: Quarters consist of canvas tents filled with bunk bed cots.
Bunkers: Concrete slabs as offshore bases' central command bunkers.
Staging: Furnish garrisons with folding metal chairs and plastic tables.

Fighting Positions

Sandbags: Artillery outposts are lined with sandbags in place of fencing.
Towers: Ladders access towers at outposts while bases rely on staircases.
Foxholes: Tag teams operate machine guns in foxholes along checkpoints.
Hedgehogs: Tank obstacles serve in place of pillboxes at their entrances.
Barrels: Adds extra weight to tents so they can resist wind and attacks.
Trenches: Connects structures protecting personnel from sharpshooters.

Observation posts outside camp outposts are dug by infantrymen.

Review

Navies

Nuclear Safety:

Foundering warships have numerous fail sales on reactors preventing detonation. Engine rooms are shielded, powerplants automatically shut down and water pressure above the ocean floor prevents sinking warships from going critical. Air blasting cannot create fallout since topsoil doesn't come into contact with our MIRV ICBMs!

Littoral Combat:

Guided destroyers are obligated to be small and agile enough to engage inshore patrol vessels. MCMVs also clear underwater obstacles too. Frigates are tasked with sailing upriver to eliminate inland river boats. Time your landings during high tide to reduce the distance amphibious IFVs travel. Smaller submarines experience greater stealth and can dive deeper. Apart from inserting SEAL Teams, they must always remain beneath the thermal layer. Travel slow around enemies to prevent bubbles.

Air Forces

The allied air forces need to study WWII and Soviet aerial combat maneuvers. Rudder yaws shrink turning radiuses. Cobra pit maneuvers force pursuers to overshoot aircraft. Immelmann loops deny radar-guided missiles the opportunity to drop down above you. Split Ss defeat heat-seekers. Giraffes ambush enemy combatants. ATCs coax enemies to move into the proper position we want and can strafe ground units.

Armies

Snipers are either commandos equipped with DMRs or tower guards manning bolt-action rifles. Gunners man LMGs to defend checkpoints. Grenadiers lead squads of infantry. Fireteam corporals breach doors with shotgun attachments. Everyone else is issued standard carbines. Fix bayonets on assault rifles and carbines during engagements. Tank and aviation crews lack SMGs; give them improved M1911s!

CHAPTER FOURTEEN
Privatized Park Systems

Quadrant 4:1

Listed below is this chapter's section directory. Topics are grouped together in subsections labeled by underlined bullets. Any further subdivision of information is organized into verses marked by bolded bullets.

Overview

Interior

Land Management:

Parks shall account for 52% of all U.S. land and 62% of territory. Farms represent 36% and civilization itself remains less than 3%. Private sector organizations can band together to form co-ops owning 99% of their total acreage! Relocate existing park locations to bottomlands bordered by ridges designated as serpentine belts. Beyond these lines lie the uplands. Mountain peaks, islands and caves are protected by PWA.

Park Administration:

Wilderness outside D.C. is devested into state parks. Ghost counties become ranges and ghost towns stations. Relocate historic buildings to serve as living quarters and bulldoze everything deemed as nonessential property. Greenhouses culture moss and mushrooms. Warehouses store seed bags and colorful water jugs. A deputy's outpost is a marina with one gas pump capable of supplying vehicles and boaters. Ranger stations offer two while game wardens get three. Judiciary rangers require an avenor, pathologist and two bailiffs. U.S. Marshals shall employ this system as well.

Regions

Wilderness Areas:

Upland preserves welcome extractive industry. Camp groups sublease bottomland refuges to visitors. Mountain bases house ski resorts permitted to thin tree density along slopes. Beachfronts and coastal islands are reserved. For sanctuaries, seagrass beds, seaweed and plankton thrive in cold climates. Mangroves, stromatolites and coral reefs excel in warmer environments. Don't forget to include underwater caves!

Resourceful Ranges:

Organizations must acquire seed bags before logging almost everything, minus virgin stands of species that belong there according to my models, once. Then, they replant the correct species and lease plots up to 5,000 acres. Seasonal burning is mandatory.

Master Template

Ecosystems

Honeycomb Grids:

Pangea separated long before Earth's current ecosystems even formed. Therefore, any plant species presenting itself in more than one continent didn't migrate across a single supercontinent. Instead, environmental factors such as climate, elevation and proximity to freshwater led to the evolution of today's current habitats. That's why Japan and the U.S. both have cherry trees. Unbeknownst to everyone, they're not two separate forests. Amazingly, both are merely part of one global ecosystem!

Jigsaw Patterns:

Plants in a bottomland forest had similar leaf shapes. Additionally, their pines had matching bark patterns too! There are three stratified aquifers. Headwaters dug down to the pebbles (1st), tributaries cobbles (2nd) and estuaries boulders (3rd). Streambeds held underwater aquatics, pools floating varieties and shorelines carnivorous bulrush controlling pestilence along shorelines. Stone is the foundation of all mountain ranges.

Terrestrial Rainbows:

Regardless of tree species, every temperate forest displays a variety of colors during autumn. Wildflowers present colorful arrays. However, everything else inside these ecosystems is color-coordinated. This applies to grass, mushrooms, moss, topsoil, clay, rocks, stones and cyanobacteria that gives freshwater its distinct color pattern!

Elevation

Mountain Ranges:

As you ascend ranges, they'll transition from a darked-colored ecosystem to a lighter one. There are three zones: Foothill, montane and alpine. Alpine streams were lined by stunted conifers and upland areas below tree lines lacking tuckamores. The latter term is defined as deformed subalpine vegetation due to wind damage. Montane regions support huge trees with big leaves. Foothills are their complete antithesis.

Microclimates:

Ecosystems inside biomes are divided by fall lines and watersheds. Rolling hills, stony bluffs or mountains often separate them. Sometimes, you could have cliffs creating microclimates for riverine oak habitats with prairie uplands. Map these habitats out beforehand. Planting species in the correct areas can prevent outbreaks of blight.

Wastelands

Upland Barrens:

Temperate forests should have up to a dozen pine species regardless of it being categorized as a subspecies, variant, etc. Only one dominates an upland. Sections of streams had serpentine belts of pine bordering their hardwood habitats, each with its own unique species. Uplands and belts are uneven-aged stands comprised of an emergent, canopy, subcanopy and understory layer. Prairies had shortgrass uplands, tallgrass belts and canebrake bottomlands. Stepping stones were havens for moss at crossings. Caves require glowing mushrooms, moss and lichens to aid navigation!

Watersheds

Mountain Streams:

Upland aquafers feed springs. Springs, sometimes in the form of hot springs, are small pools babbling into brooks. Brooks fall into gullies, which are drop-offs feeding ponds. Ponds, sometimes in the form of geysers, are medium-sized pools bleeding towards rapids. Rapids cascade down waterfalls to be greeted by even larger pools called lakes. These lakes funnel water through mouths before it reaches the fjords.

Coastal Flatwoods:

Pine barrens' aquafers feed small pools known as springs. Springs carve rills. Rills bleed over creeks. Creeks feed medium-sized pools called ponds. Ponds spill towards rivers. Rivers widen into deltas supplying tidal lakes, which exit through mouths. Manmade masonry replenishes rock beds and stepping stones along stream banks.

Prairie Grasslands:

Prairie watersheds come in two flavors: Alpine meadows or plains. The plains system uses my flatwoods model, but replaces pools with three kinds of marshes. Three sizes of wetlands range from miniature seeps, to mid-sized wallows and oversized fens. Tidal marshes are often brackish in nature, meaning freshwater mixes with saltwater.

Lowland Aquifers:

Stop quarries from depleting rock beds along these watersheds! From now on, landscaping wholesalers are supplied masonry responsibly sourced from our uplands This includes everything from stone, rock, clay, sand, topsoil, potting mixes and worm castings. Without these rock beds, our rivers suffer erosion and decreased sanitation.

Pristine Waters:

Water color is determined by bacteria. Each ecosystem harbored certain species. This helps stabilize PH and potability. When introducing cultures add so little that water remains crystal clear. It needs to be translucent enough so campers can see the bottom of streambeds or pools. Larger bodies showcase an obvious colorful hue.

Bottomlands

Unmixed Forests:

Temperate categories include hardwood, coniferous or oasis. Hardwood tiers are tree, shrub, bush and carpet. Desert uplands combine cacti badlands with palm oases. Valleys in canyons cradle xeric hardwood forests along their riparian sections.

Tributary Transitions:

Total quantity of species, number of leaf blades, overall size and showiness fades the further upriver you travel. Headwaters could behave deciduous, tributaries semi-deciduous, channels semi-evergreen and estuaries evergreen in certain regions. Softwoods, such as conifers and pine, act deciduous as they near alpine headwaters!

Forest Flooring:

Serpentine belts also have their own lists of grass and wildflowers. Flowering vines climbed emergent trees, liverworts encircled the bases of most canopy varieties, hornworts surrounded understory brush and moss provided walkways. Fallen logs created openings for lichens. Spanish moss and mistletoe fulfill similar roles in other forests. Toadstools colonized tree stumps and assisted in decomposing hardwoods.

Aquatic Vegetation:

Marshes have flowering grass. Underwater aquatics follow the same transition rules. Plant shorter species at tributaries and run taller ones along major estuaries. Fan boats access waterways to inspect beavers' dams and eliminate potential blockages. Prescribing seasonal burns along wetlands is more difficult due to moisture levels. Wait until grass grows tall, plants turn brown and water levels recede before burning.

Wetlands

Climax Succession:

Mires are wetlands clogged by heavy peat deposits due to fire suppression. Yet, overharvesting can damage them too. Marshes become bogs and pools swampland. Bogs: A muskeg is found in colder climates, quagmires overtake warmer zones and moors exist within the xeric regions. Swamp vegetation: Carrs are bushy, pocosins shrubby and sloughs wooded. Jungles are overgrown upland habitats inside forests.

Restoration Efforts:

Reintroduce rare animal species back to their habitats once everything is restored. DARPA helps scientists restore extinct species back to life! U.S. military bases fire biodegradable bombs and artillery shells to initiate avalanches and prescribe seasonal controlled burns. CCC personnel convert urban channels to greenway trails. Streams within communities and neighborhoods are managed by HOAs. As for park rangers, drone patrols reduce poaching and helicopters perform rescue missions.

Establishing Piers

Bays

Badland Areas:

Badlands contain steep cliffs called bights. They're fairly shallow, yet still deeper than sounds. Sometimes these cliffs wander in-and-out like a meandering river. Coastal coves are small, crescent-shaped, coastal recesses with their own protected beaches. Many of the terms below, especially coves, are used to describe areas of inland lakes.

Montane Highlands:

Some mountainous rivers might end at a lake. Others press onward through fjords. The latter are deep, channels surrounded by steep mountains. As deltas broaden and become mouths, the final sections of them that connect to the sea are called firths.

Flatwoods Floodplains:

Flatwoods have that sound! They're rather shallow and often brackish as a result of freshwater mixing with saltwater. Acidity keeps streams clean and is an ideal PH for plants. Alkalinity prevents red tides in oceans. For coastal prairie ecosystems, rivers in grasslands and tundra environments are linked to oceans via numerous sounds.

Coastal Islands:

Atolls are ring-shaped barrier islands. Sandbars separate warm, shallow, colorful waters of lagoons from the high seas. Spits only connect one side while shoals joint two or more. Manmade jetties serve as breakwaters to disrupt storm surges. Isthmuses linking an island to the shore are tombolos. Straights happen to be natural geographical landmasses while manmade canals contain locks. Land bridges connect continents together. Prime examples include the Bering, Panama and Suez straights.

Berths

Ideal Inlets:

Towns and cities should have at least one local park with a pond to skip rocks across. There are two types of harbors: Marinas and ports. State parks build marinas in lakefront coves. Boats should get slips, piers, dock ties and boat houses. Coastal fishing towns do the same thing. Ports have similar facilities. Shipyards construct new assets. Spillways launch ships, berths perform repairs, wharfs handle boarding and bollards anchor mooring ties. Over time, ports grew into major coastal cities and began dominating entire bays. Spain even named a red wine after the word too!

Urban Interface

Municipal

Freedom Towers:

The Big Apple's twin towers were replaced by the One World Trade Center and 9/11 Memorial. Having only one building is more economical than two. Coincidentally, replacing outdated high-rises with a handful of taller skyscrapers benefits us two ways. First, it lets us consolidate numerous tight, one-way roads down to spacious two-way streets lined with tree planters. Second, it justifies the construction of a second Freedom Tower! My plan encourages NYC's city council market municipal bonds to cover these expenditures. All other municipalities should also follow suit.

Business Corridors:

Keep highway medians and verges open to the point they resemble grasslands. Underpasses adopt flowers. Interchanges plant local understories along retention basins. Loops, avenues, parking alleys and boulevards apply the same principle above, but feature additional subcanopy tree planters in front of business centers.

Pedestrian Villages:

Deed restrictions mandate home owners shroud three sides of their property, two if lakefront or on a golf course, with a mixed hardwood forest comprised of regional species. Pedestrian villages inspired my towns to do the same. Fences between two backyards butt one another, yet each side still has its own greenbelt. Underground power, natural gas, city water, sewage and 5G WIFI become the industry standard!

Township

Civil Townships:

Town councils encourage locals to migrate inward within their limits via temporary property tax relief. Businesses move to junctions while farm smallholdings line town loops. Raceways deliver emergency water supplies from their central water towers.

Rural Countryside:

Professional family farms exist outside cities and towns. Hardwoods freely line all driveways and houses. Osage oranges are perfect for subsections like watering holes. Mixed hardwoods separate major and minor sections from each other while doubling as windbreaks to prevent potential dust bowls from happening. Pine barrens along property lines provide adequate privacy and can survive the fiercest of droughts.

Review

Public

Seed Libraries:

NSF vessels trade seeds with other countries, regardless of political standing. Jailbirds print license plates and remove litter. Prisoners work in chain gangs within state parks. Inmates recover seeds, fungal spores and bacteria cultures for water jugs. Pathologists identify species and segregate them into bags. Staff distribute them to loggers so they can replant logged plots. Anyone is welcome to buy these seed bags!

Quarantining Blights:

American Chestnut was originally a minor component in beech forests confined to montane deltas. Native Americans expanded it across Appalachia beyond its native habitat. Thus, it fell victim to blight. Ash in the Great Lakes and elm in the Eastern Seaboard suffered a similar fate. Upon collecting all available seeds, log everything in the uplands. Destroy all infected timber during prescribed burns. Environmental conditions continue segregating afflicted species from various unaffected sections.

Private

Scorched Earth:

Civilians remove invasive species. Give them bounties in the form of tax credits. Encourage them to market their goods as affordable products to consumers. Timber should be converted to affordable firewood or future modern biodiesel additives. Invasive sea life includes Asian carp, lionfish, green crabs and zebra mussels. Create delicious meals from these nuisances for working class folk at local bars if need be!

Thinning Herds:

Feel free to thin groves of Osage orange, hackberry, box elder, sweetgum, green ash, vines and even pine when they become too thick. Plant carnivorous bulrush along ditches to control mosquito populations. Demolish all derelict buildings for safety reasons and so property appears less creepy. Backfill every abandoned mineshaft.

CHAPTER FIFTEEN

The Planet's Ecosystems

<u>Quadrant 4:2</u>

Listed below is this chapter's section directory. Topics are grouped together in subsections labeled by underlined bullets. Any further subdivision of information is organized into verses marked by bolded bullets.

Overview

Biosphere

Four Elements:

Earth's biosphere is comprised of its lithosphere (earth), hydrosphere (water), atmosphere (air) and biosphere (ecosystems). My Master Template has two realms for all its vegetation, both floral and fungal. Realms split into biomes. Biomes are groupings of plant ecosystems. Ecosystems subdivide into sections called habitats.

Holarctic Elevation:

Our planet's Northern Hemisphere is the Holarctic and southern Perennial realms. Taiga, woodland and savanna biomes dominate the former. Evolution was influenced by elevation. The first two always have subalpine, montane, foothill and flatwoods ecosystems. Woodlands have floodplains, not canyons. Savanna ecosystems are thinner and composed of heathland, scrubland, chaparral, sandhills and canyons. Pine is absent in canyons' serpentine belts and floodplains lack uplands in general.

Perennial Realty:

Hardwoods, fern trees, palms and bamboo behave two ways: Semi-deciduous in higher elevation cloud forests while retaining most of their leaves, albeit displaying color until springtime. Or, semi-evergreen where some leaves shed and a few change colors. Since everything retains its foliage annually, I've named it the Perennial realm!

Biomes

Interior Grasslands:

Mountains generated microclimates leading to the formation of desert badlands and forests. Without them, our planet would be nothing more than prairie grassland and a pair of polar ice caps. Every ecosystem contains carnivorous bulrush along its shores to reduce pestilence and vermin. Some are large enough to consume small animals. Canebrakes, itself a form of bamboo, doubles as windbreaks letting farmers prevent potential dust storms from destroying their plots. After all, erosion degrades topsoil.

116

Holarctic Realm

Taiga Biome

Lodgepole Pine Forest: Subalpine

Requires limber/whitebark pines, larch, spruce, fir, yellowwood, totara – white.

White Pine Forest: Montane

Plant Asian pines, aspen, birch, alder, tallow, cottonwood, sycamore – platinum.

Red Pine Forest: Foothill

Lacebark, knobcone and red pine subgenus. Cherry, myrtle, beautyberry – silver.

Grey Pine Forest: Flatwoods

Prime examples include Jack pine, white oak, hawthorn, dusty miller – light green.

Hedgehog Cactus Desert: Canyon

Cacti badlands, succulent belts, tanoak, madrone, sagebrush bottomlands – black.

Woodland Biome

Pitch Pine Forest: Subalpine

Table mountain, pond and spruce pines sprout needles directly out of their trunks. Needs yew, hemlock, podocarpus, phyllocladus and prumnopitys conifers – blue hues.

Shortleaf Pine Forest: Montane

Virginia/stone pines, maple, sweetgum, tulip poplar, hazel, hydrangea – indigo. Sourwood belongs in the red pine forest because its leaves are similar to cherry trees.

Longleaf Pine Forest: Foothill

Caribbean pine, beech, hornbeam, elm, hophornbeam, chestnut, buckeye – pink. Native Americans from the New World discovered cannabis residing in these forests!

Slash Pine Forest: Flatwoods

Give it Central American, loblolly and sand pines. Red oaks, wormwood – green. Let's broaden the definition of black oak to include the deciduous half of red oak species!

Tupelo Forest: Floodplain

Run tupelo, pawpaw, basswood, catalpa, magnolia, laurel, sassafras – purple. There are no serpentine belts or uplands. Therefore, there are no pine barrens present.

Savanna Biome

Bristlecone Pine Forest: Heathland

Add foxtail pines. Juniper, cedar, cypress, sequoia and redwoods too. Incorporates monkey puzzle, Afrocarpus, dacrydium, dacrycarpus and nageia conifers – yellow.

Ponderosa Pine Forest: Scrubland

Southwestern pine belts. Walnut, hickory, ash, locust, mesquite, sumac – orange. Toothache trees, Hercules' clubs, prickly ash and partridge peas line its understory.

Piñon Pine Forest: Chaparral

Piñon pine serpentine belts, willows, St. John's Wort, wild rice aquatics – brown. Few realize these pine and willow species showcase a rainbow of colors in their foliage!

Black Pine Forest: Sandhill

Californian/Mediterranean pines, evergreen oak, holly, teaberry – dark green. Let's broaden the definition of live oak to include all evergreens in the red oak subgenus!

Barrel Cactus Desert: Canyon

Cacti badlands, succulent belts, stone oak/manzanita/olive bottomlands – red.

Grassland Biome

Tundra: Arctic Meadow

Permafrost inhibits all but heath along arctic plains. Includes alpine meadows.

Steppe: Montane Field

Mongolia, the Silk Road and California Valley are dry, mountainous grasslands.

Prairie: Interior Plain

The Sahara was once like the Great Plains! A true desert has badland plateaus.

Bulrush: Riparian Shoreline

Listed in order of biomes: Waterwheel, corkscrew, sundew and bladderwort.

Coastal Biome

Dome: Palm Hammock

Feather (tropical) and fan (subtropical) palms dominate oases and beaches.

Shelf: Tidal Range

Layers: Seagrass/mangroves, seaweed/stromatolites and plankton/coral reefs.

Perennial Realm

Rainforests

Floodplain Biome: Lowland

Rainforests and bushlands are two of the Perennial realm's subrealms. Fan palm barrens once monopolized upland regions before fire suppression introduced climax succession. Feather palms line their desert oases and coastal hammocks. Fern trees created serpentine belts bordering their watersheds' bottomland hardwood forests.

Cloud Forest Biome: Highland

Montane vegetation is similar to my aforementioned flood basins above. Subalpine elevation is home to the foggy, bamboo highlands. They become increasingly stunted towards alpine headwaters. Bamboo isn't a tree, it's a type of grass! It lets waterways cast shade over weary travelers. Neighboring uplands are lined by open meadows.

Bushland

Savanna Biome: Veldt

Tons of pine species exist outside the genus *Pinus*! Pine dominated upland barrens and serpentine belts bordering xeric hardwood forests at bottomlands. Overgrowth examples: Brambles (vines), brush (bushes), hedgerows (shrubs) and thickets (trees).

Desert Biome: Outback

Ecosystems mirror Holarctic badlands. Plateau uplands cradled cacti. Stones held clumps of grass, flowers and smaller species. Sporadic taller cacti were out in the open. Serpentine belts held succulents while bottomlands were hardwood forests.

Grassland Biome: Pampas

Varying elevation led to the same alpine meadow, montane field, interior plain and riparian shoreline ecosystems encountered in our Northern Hemisphere. South Africa first coined the term veldt, Australia desert outback and Argentina pampas!

Bulrush

My definition of bulrush is not to be confused with the genus *Schoenoplectus*. Carrion flowers control vermin and pestilence along floodplains. Pitcher plants were common in subalpine climates. Venus flytraps originated in Perennial brushland environments. Carolinian populations migrated north through Southern Florida from the tropics.

Review

Discovery

Virgin Forestry:

After the last ice age ended, receding glaciers carved out Appalachia and the Ozarks. As ice melted, it eventually created the Mississippi River, which split the three belts of ranges right in two. Certain areas were home to canyons, hence the presence of prickly pear cacti out east. Once Native Americans crossed the Bering Strait, they began cultivating the land and started trading seeds between neighboring tribesmen.

Old-growth Stands:

Caves were scraped of their colorful moss and iridescent fungi. Fuel was burnt for warmth while cave paintings were drawn. Tribes thinned unproductive species and expanded those deemed valuable. Thus, American Chestnut began dominating Appalachia! Unfortunately, planting them outside the habitats they were adapted to weakened them to blight. Natives mistook longleaf pine in foothills as a superior, slower-growing version of slash pine in the flatwoods because it had similar bark.

Recovery

Central Hardwoods:

Magnolias and laurels are salt-resistant evergreens lining shorelines. Further upriver beyond basswoods lie shorter, more deciduous tupelos. Restored tidal lakes lack underwater groves of cypress or tupelo trees! Boost cypress populations along xeric subalpine waters before clearing stands. Now, everyone has cleaner water and less pestilence! The Central Hardwood Forest is devoid of any serpentine belts or uplands.

Oak Savannas:

Terrain can create conditions combining a grassy upland with a bottomland oak habitat. Yet. It still qualifies as a savanna once you average out overall tree density throughout the ecosystem. Anything westward beyond FDR shelterbelts should only have tallgrass as belts and canebrakes along streams. So, clear and burn seasonally!

Summary

Mission Debriefing

Recap

This concludes my presentation of *Saving the United States*, the ultimate handbook on all things public sector! This plan wasn't geared solely for local politicians wanting to change government, it's for your people too! They must possess this knowledge so we can inform our leaders and inspect their work according to my literature. Participants need to understand how to balance the political lean in their country. Shifting party support lets natives decide what legislation passes or gets blocked.

Rehash

There'll be time periods where you'll need to read portions of this book again. Operation White Wolf is spread across three generations. It's only natural to rehash on certain topics, especially when answering questions or imparting this wisdom to your future offspring. Although our enemies wouldn't do the same for us, never rip anyone off. Tribal politicians should stash a copy of my literature in their offices. Natives ought to do the same during rallies. Guard these secrets with your own life!

Closing

The next step is to finish reading TAX TREES' second volume: *Native American Strategies*. This sequel guides readers through my business portion of my plan. It contains everything from spiritual wisdom, diet and exercise, budget planning, outcompeting rivals at getting hired, furthering education and entrepreneurial practices. As principal investigator and sole researcher of this project, I'm signing off now. If you still need more resources, feel free to read my online bibliographies!

Conclusion

Afterword

Thank you for reading his book! When Robert started this project, he lacked a government grant or research team to aid him in his efforts. This man wasn't gainfully-employed for over a decade due to mental health problems. Food stamps was all he had and no other financial aid was available while conducting research. The author was forced to live off less than $100 a week.

Your support not only furthers this author's research, but also helps the indigenous people throughout the New World finally have a chance to break free from these Germanic/Anglo-Saxon civilizations destroying their countries.

-N.D.

Postface

TAX TREES began as TREES FOR TAXES, a tax-deductible landscaping program. It encouraged locals residing in Montgomery County, TX to replant native species on their property to combat the urbanization destroying our forests. After that failed, it became the Landscaper's Bible, a forestry research book.

I also tried offering the American people a plan on how to pay off the U.S. national debt, but no one cared. Afterwards, I knew I had to do something. So, I decided it was time to help the natives remove these idiots off their land!

-R.R.

Acknowledgements

I would like to thank GOTCHA! LLP for editorial services and Kindle Direct Publishing for publishing my books. Special thanks to Streetlight Graphics who designed the signature "money tree" illustrations on my monogram pages.

Special mention to Unsplash.com for allowing their digital photography to used in my works. Each photographer will be given recognition on my website. My bibliographies list the websites I've drawn information from as sources.

I personally thank everyone who read my first book! Most importantly, I give God credit for everything. If it weren't for his divine guidance, I would've never succeeded in creating these models if I tried relying solely on my own efforts. Blessed be those who partake in Operation White Wolf and support my work.

Saving the United States

"The handbook that teaches Native Americans how to save the United States, take back their country and banish the non-native traitors forever!"

CONTRIBUTIONS

Subsection Index

About the Author

My name is Robert Robinson. I began life as a cowboy working on my family's ranch. As I reached middle school, I joined the Civil Air Patrol. The U.S. Air Force's auxiliary interested me so much that I began studying military history. During high school, I opened a landscaping business and named it Robinson's Landscaping. It was never legally-registered nor did it ever hire more than two employees, most of the time only serving as temporary help.

I was awarded two degrees in applied science at The Art Institute of Houston after graduating from the Class of '05 at Montgomery High School (MISD) in Montgomery, Texas. The first certificate was my Associate of Restaurant Catering and Management. Upon returning, I earned a bachelor's degree in Hospitality Management. During my time in the industry, I worked as a line cook, prep cook, expeditor (expo), waiter, host, busser and delivery driver.

Afterwards, I focused on my research to save Western civilization. I've played drums since the year 2000 and am an avid music enthusiast. I also diet and weight train as a form of physical rehabilitation, something I've had to do twice from being drugged and bewitched by others. I'm using my experience and research in lieu of education to touch on these post-doctoral topics.

Glossary

AA Weapons

Anti-aircraft, aka ack-ack. It's an acronym describing most anti-aircraft defenses. Guns surpassing 20-40mm are labelled flak cannons instead of ack-ack. According to the U.S. Navy, anything between 3-5" dual-purpose weapons. Both serves as artillery against ships or vehicles, and as modern-day AA platforms alongside aerial missiles.

ABM Systems

Anti-ballistic missiles. These ballistic missiles are intended to shoot down incoming nuclear missiles or waves of cruise missiles. Gatling guns eliminate bomb threats. Our military's ballistic defense grid requires these ballistic defense missiles – a synonym.

Accessories (Items)

An aiguillette was a rope on a knight's shoulder used to secure their breastplate. Lanyards are either lacey rings of rope on one's shoulder or necklaces dangling items, such as USB flash drives, car keys, ID cards, training whistles, digital stopwatches, etc.

Apparel (Covers)

A digger hat is an Australian-style cap with one side pinned up in place. Campaign hats are what most people usually saw American drill sergeants wearing. Side caps are tent-shaped covers worn with dress uniforms. Forage caps can denote female officers or cooks. Peaked caps can be best described as a general's or policeman's lid.

Artillery Shells

Some shells create FLAK (aerial explosions) in the sky, but weren't considered true FLAK guns due to their girth. Tanks fire SABOTs (shoe-wrapped, fin-stabilized explosive rods) at other MBTs. HEAT (high-explosive anti-tank) rounds destroy armored units.

Brevity Codes

Prior to launch, operators broadcast, "Fox-1" if it's a semi-guided radar missile requiring a lock the entire time. Announcing "Fox-2" is meant for heat-seekers. "Fox-3" is shouted before firing fire-and-forget radar-guided missiles. Yelling "Fox-4", aka guns-guns-guns, during close-ranged dogfights means a gunfight is about to happen.

Cannon Calibers

Cannon calibers require at least a 20mm diameter. Navies define small batteries as anything under 5", lights 5-6", heavies 7-8" and large calibers above 9". For army artillery, think of light batteries as 4" or under, mediums 4-6" and heavies above 6".

Close-in Weapons Systems

Phalanxes are close-in weapons systems (CISWs) aboard naval ships as a final line of defense (point-defense) against descending projectiles or swarms of boarding craft.

Countermeasures

Chaff is aluminum-coats glass jettisoned to disrupt incoming radar-guided missiles. Flares disrupt heat-seeking ordinance. Electronic countermeasures (ECM pods) jam enemy targeting equipment. Ships drop sonar decoys (noise makers) underwater to confuse homing torpedoes. Lasers disrupt missiles' guidance systems, but are costly.

Machine Guns

Automatic rifles served as squad automatic weapons (SAWs) until three, portable machine guns came into existence: Light machineguns (LMG), medium machineguns (MMG) and heavy machineguns (HMG). General purpose MMGs can double as SAWs.

Missile Categories

AGMs are air-to-ground missiles designed for aircraft. SSMs represent surface-to-ship missiles given to warships and coastal batteries. UGM means underwater-guided missile letting subs sink surface combatants. Cruise missiles are given to warships, cargo planes, and coastal MLRS. Nuclear versions are the most discreet way to attack.

Rocket Launchers

Handheld recoilless rifles are rocket launchers and come in three sizes: Light (LAW), medium (MAW) and heavy (HAW). The last option is almost always guided making it a missile launcher. Our man-portable air defense systems (MPADs) can fire Stingers.

SAM Batteries

Surface-to-air missiles. SAM sites can be land-based MLRS batteries or launchers mounted on warships. Ground forces have short-ranged heat-seekers to down enemy helicopters. Naval assets prefer medium to long-ranged radar-guided pods.

SEAD Missions

Suppression of enemy air defenses. Missions entail fighter jets destroying ground targets in the form of SAMs, aircraft, etc. Anti-radiation missiles (ARMs) detect emissions without using active radar. ECM pods jam enemy detection equipment. HARM is an acronym for high-speed anti-radiation missile and are used by the U.S.

Smalls Arms Fire

Small arms include everything below 20mm. Anything wider is a cannon. HP stands for hollow-point, SJHP semi-jacketed hollow-point, JHP jacketed hollow point, FMJ full-metal jacket and AP armor-piercing. SLAP rounds incorporate tungsten sabots and C4 incendiary warheads. Anti-material stands for anti-vehicle or anti-armor.

Colophon

Graphic Design Group

Graphic Design, Covers

TAX TREES: THE LANDSCAPER'S BIBLE, (ed. 3)

TAX TREES: SAVING THE UNITED STATES, (ed. 1)

TAX TREES: NATIVE AMERCIAN STRATEGIES, (ed. 1)

Kindle Direct Publishing

Publishing, Marketing

TAX TREES: technical handbook trilogy (ed. 1-2)

BJÖRK'S ADVENTURE, parody thriller novel (ed. 1)

MY DIRE STRAITS, author's memoir (ed. 1-2)

CANNABIS MARKET, technical handbook (ed. 1)

THE EARLY CHURCH, technical handbook (ed. 1)

BEER MATH, technical handbook (ed. 1)

Amazon.com, Inc.

Printing, Distribution

TAX TREES: THE LANDSCAPER'S BIBLE, (ed. 1-3)

TAX TREES, technical handbook trilogy (ed. 1)

BJÖRK'S ADVENTURE, parody thriller novel (ed. 1)

MY DIRE STRAITS, author's memoir (ed. 1)

CANNABIS MARKET, technical handbook (ed. 1)

THE EARLY CHURCH, technical handbook (ed. 1)

2012 Copyright: TXU 1-821-070

https://robertrobinsonjr.com

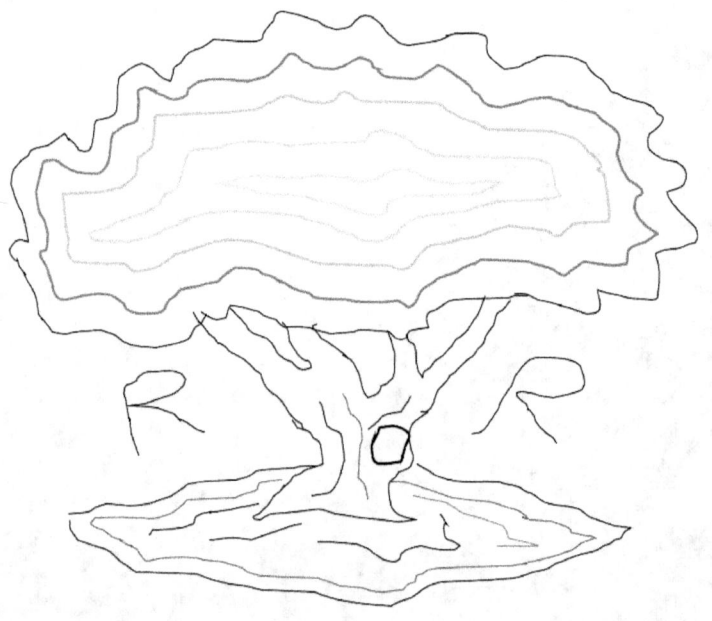

www.ingramcontent.com/pod-product-compliance
Lightning Source LLC
Chambersburg PA
CBHW072143280526
45788CB00002B/763